26 F E E T *to the*
CHARLOTTES

26 FEET *to the* CHARLOTTES

Exploring the Land of the Haida

▶ JUNE CAMERON

VICTORIA • VANCOUVER • CALGARY

Heritage House Publishing Company Ltd.
#108 – 17665 66A Avenue
Surrey, BC V3S 2A7
www.heritagehouse.ca

Heritage House Publishing Company Ltd.
PO Box 468
Custer, WA
98240-0468

Library and Archives Canada Cataloguing in Publication

Cameron, June, 1929–
26 feet to the Charlottes: exploring the land of the Haida / June Cameron.

ISBN 978-1-894974-61-5

    1. Cameron, June, 1929–　　—Travel—British Columbia—Queen Charlotte Islands.
2. Queen Charlotte Islands (B.C.)—Description and travel. 3. Sailing—British Columbia—
Queen Charlotte Islands. I. Title. II. Title: Twenty-six feet to the Charlottes.

FC3845.Q3C35 2009　　　917.11'12044　　　C2009-900089-X

Library of Congress Control Number: 2009920204

Edited by Audrey McClellan
Proofread by Karla Decker
Cover design by Jacqui Thomas
Interior design and layout by Darlene Nickull
Cover photos by John Alexander (top) and June Cameron

Printed in Canada

Heritage House acknowledges the financial support for its publishing program from the Government of Canada through the Book Publishing Industry Development Program (BPIDP), Canada Council for the Arts, and the province of British Columbia through the British Columbia Arts Council and the Book Publishing Tax Credit.

The Canada Council | Le Conseil des Arts
for the Arts | du Canada

BRITISH COLUMBIA
ARTS COUNCIL
Supported by the Province of British Columbia

This book was produced on 100% post-consumer recycled paper, processed chlorine free and printed with vegetable-based dyes.

This book is for my cousin Rod Griffin

ACKNOWLEDGEMENTS

Without Paul Holsinger's courage and wonderful mechanical ability, this adventure could never have happened. The fact that he has had to wait 25 years to see it in print is a testament to his amazing patience. I needed that much time to understand the significance of the many relics of First Nations culture we stumbled upon as we meandered up this wild coastline.

When I was struggling with the research, it was my cousin Rod who answered my queries with 12-page handwritten accounts of the coast he knows so well from having ventured into its every nook and cranny and worked in both the logging and fishing industries. His memories could fill several books beyond the three that I have written.

But when all is said and done, it is my editor, Audrey McClellan, who deserves the greatest accolade, for without her skilful trimming and tidying, this book may have become no more than a long-winded travelogue. I hope it brings my readers as much satisfaction as the writing of it has brought me.

A final note: To retain the flavour of the time when I made the trip described in this book, I refer to places by the names they had a quarter-century ago and use terms that were acceptable at that time.

CONTENTS

INTRODUCTION

We were 13 days out of Vancouver on our way to the Queen Charlotte Islands, just about to leave the sheltered waters of the Inside Passage for a crossing of treacherous Hecate Strait, when a vicious northwesterly gale stalled us. This nasty bit of weather kept us holed up for three days in an uninspiring cove in the lee of Pitt Island.

On the fourth day, the wind moderated and we ventured out. It felt good to be beating our way upcoast again. We were sailing. The sun was shining. What more could a sailor ask? Fewer swells would have been nice, but the wind was down to around 15 knots, and our little wooden sloop, *Wood Duck*, blazed away with me at the helm and Paul tidying up lines and making things secure.

I was used to racing my own sailboat in worse weather, so this was no real challenge, although Paul's boat, with its full keel, handled differently than did my 24-foot San Juan with its short fin keel. But *Wood Duck* chewed purposefully into the waves. Whenever we were hit by a sudden gust, I spilled excess air by heading into the wind, and the boat straightened up. We both grinned at the progress we were making on our journey.

Then, with a crack, the forestay pulled loose from the bow of the boat and the genoa flew off to one side with a roar of flailing cloth. I instinctively turned the hull to follow the sail, thereby saving the mast.

We watched in horror as the writhing sail billowed ahead of us with the metal strap thrashing at the end. The mast was still standing and the mainsail pulled us forward drunkenly as we ran down the faces of the waves. The roller furling line still held one corner of the huge foresail, and the sheets (the ropes leading to the winches) held the other, so Paul let the sheets go to ease the strain and flatten out the sail while I clung to the helm, trying to keep the boat from turning broadside. We had to keep the nose downwind if we were to save the mast.

The following sea lifted our stern and whitecaps hissed as they boiled alongside. By the time the foot of Pitt Island was abeam, Paul had managed to haul the sail down and jury-rig a temporary headstay so we could tack into the shelter of the island and make our way back to the anchorage. The miracle was that he managed all this without going overboard.

◀ ▶

In 1983, when Paul Holsinger and I set out to sail to the Queen Charlotte Islands in his old 26-foot wooden sloop, we knew that we were taking on a major challenge. But neither of us was aware of how much danger we actually faced. We had grown confident in our survival skills after spending the previous three summers exploring the BC coast as far north as Ocean Falls. We were a water-wise, compatible, middle-aged couple who shared, among other things, an interest in fishing and beachcombing. But all of our trips so far had been in fairly sheltered waters. All that was about to change.

In order to reach these offshore islands, we had to cross the notoriously dangerous Hecate Strait, with no chance of shelter for over 70 miles. This is not usually a problem in a fast boat if the skipper anticipates moderate weather, but it is a major undertaking in a small craft making only four and a half nautical miles per hour. Another problem was our lack of electronic navigational aides. They were either too expensive for our budget or had not yet been invented. In hindsight, I realize that ignorance was bliss. Not only were we unaware of the problems we faced, but we also lacked any real knowledge of what to expect once we arrived.

We knew that we would find none of the original settlements occupied, except perhaps Masset and Skidegate. And the people who lived there nowadays were likely thoroughly modern. But we wanted to visit old village sites so that we could get an idea of the challenges the original inhabitants had faced. When we finally reached the ancient village of Ninstints on Anthony Island, we discovered that collectors had taken the best of the carved poles, while rain and encroaching trees were doing their utmost to reclaim the rest. Even so, what we saw was enough to pique our interest in a culture that had produced haunting totem poles and unusual house structures in such an isolated place. The biggest mystery was how they had managed to keep warm, find food, preserve their history, stay healthy and just plain survive in this remote and unforgiving place.

I kept careful diaries during our travels because I liked to read these accounts later, on rainy winter evenings. But at that stage of my life I had no idea that I would someday write a book about these adventures. As the years passed, curiosity kept me searching for information about the places we visited and about the indigenous people who had created the art forms we saw and those we could no longer see because they amounted to little more than bulges under the moss. Unlike the stone carvings in Europe, which had suffered from bombardment during wars, these artfully created cedar structures had mostly decayed and returned to the earth from which they came. Some had been removed to museums before they and the people they represented nearly vanished in the "war" between cultures that so decimated the civilization that created them.

With the arrival of the fur traders, the Native people had access to metal tools, cooking pots, foodstuffs and such things as rope and fishing tackle, so there was no longer the need to make things with cedar, yew or stone. Fortunately the craving for beauty did not die, but the need for money to purchase all these handy items drew many of these folk into the logging and fishing industries and also kept the artisans busy, for they had found a ready market amongst the newcomers for things like miniature totem poles carved from quick-hardening argillite, bracelets moulded from silver dollars, and baskets that were still being made by a few of the older women.

During our short visit in 1983, we were too far south to see the ugly naked hillsides that were the result of clear-cut logging. Current thinking by lumbering companies was that they should remove all growth and replant with just one kind of tree. All competing species were to be eliminated by spraying with herbicides. The erosion produced by road building and clear-cutting caused streams and rivers to silt up, killing the salmon fry. The Haida Nation and environmentalists from around the world began a vigorous campaign challenging these practices, and ultimately established Gwaii Haanas National Park Reserve and Haida Heritage Site on Moresby Island.

A secondary outcome of all this activity was an upsurge in tourism. Kayakers and large cruisers came to explore these waterways but, luckily for us, Paul and I visited in a peaceful time with no worries except catching our food, finding supplies of fresh water and fuel, and avoiding rocks, storms or accidents. We were seeking adventure, and that was what we got.

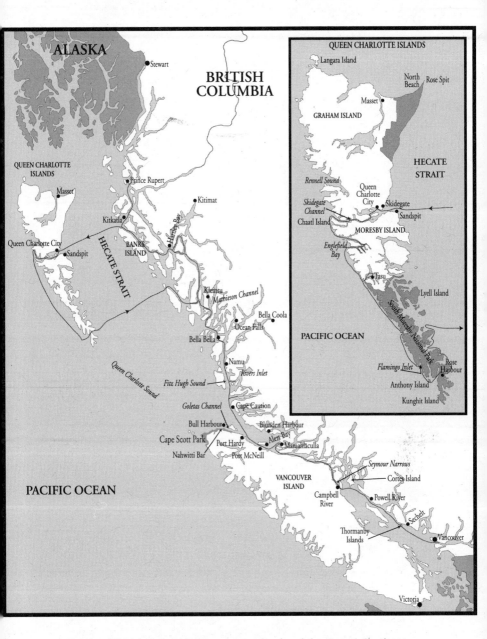

Mainland British Columbia, Vancouver Island and the Queen Charlotte Islands; place names appear as they were known at the time of the author's trip, which is shown with a dotted line.

1 GETTING TO KNOW YOU

It was storm conditions that drove Paul and me together in the first place. By coincidence both of us taught school on the Lower Mainland of British Columbia and spent our summers around Cortes Island, at the northern end of the Strait of Georgia, although we had never met.

In the summer of 1979, like all who truly enjoy their holidays, we had both put off returning to the city until the last minute. My sailing partner Michelle James and I had provisioned at Westview, near Powell River, before heading around the north end of Texada Island to see that part of the coast for the first time. But the gentle southeaster that greeted us in the morning blossomed into a real beat. We waved as we passed a pretty little sailboat that was slugging its way under power through the increasing slop. The ride got more uncomfortable, so we decided to quit early and sought shelter in landlocked Scotty Bay at the north end of Lasqueti Island. It turned out to be a wise choice. By evening the bay was plugged full of boats, and overnight the winds ranged up to 72 knots. The rigging screamed and sleep was impossible, but the muddy bottom of that tree-fringed cove saved most of us from dragging our hooks.

I found out later that it was Paul we had waved to as he did the trip all by himself in his boat, *Wood Duck*. He said that he thought my boat, *Saffron*, was crewed by a nasty husband who cruelly sent his slim little wife forward to change sails as the weather deteriorated. That was Michelle, who was a pro on the foredeck, having mastered that position during our years of racing. We were long out of sight when Paul, too, sought shelter in a nearby bay.

The wind raged on all the next day. By the third day it had eased, but the waves still came at us like shifting mountains. Time was running out for getting back to the city, so Michelle and I ventured forth in the direction of Secret Cove, a little farther down the coast, where we could leave the boat and catch a bus to Vancouver. However, when we tried to get there, we found that the waves and the wind were out of sync. The waves came around Thormanby Island, but the wind came through the gap between Thormanby and the mainland. With these conditions we could make good time on one tack and literally stall in the other direction. When the futility of the situation dawned on us, we reluctantly turned tail and ran downwind to nearby Pender Harbour, taking shelter at a marina in Hospital Bay. The bay rapidly filled with other boats in the same fix, and among them was Paul.

We first noticed him when we went dock prowling before cooking our dinner. It was the charming little wooden sloop that first caught my eye. We stopped to talk to the skipper about his boat and also about the awful weather. I could see that he was exhausted, so we invited him over for a cocktail and to share our meal. Imagine my surprise when I found out that he regularly spent the summer months near Cortes Bay, which had been my mecca for as long as I can remember.

Paul's relaxed manner and ready smile soon had me feeling as though I had known him for a long time. He was a tall, slim, silver-haired man and a boater like me. I saw in him a chance to go exploring the coast with someone closer to my own age. And, like so many lonely women, I immediately began building mental castles. Was this the Prince Charming that I sought? Before many weeks had passed, I was spending weekends with him in Richmond, where he lived and worked, but our time together was frequently interrupted by my racing. I was so totally hooked on the sport that it dominated my life. Fortunately, Paul had enough hobbies that he kept himself occupied much of the time that I was away and, because he loved sailing, he was supportive of my obsession. But in the long run, it contributed to the undoing of our relationship.

Like me, Paul longed to explore the BC coast, so before the winter was over we were already planning our first trip together. We needed to get to trust each other's skills and we needed to know what his boat could handle. *Wood Duck* was the logical choice for our travels. It was longer than my racing sailboat, and every foot of length gives you greater space inside. Two and a half feet doesn't seem like much, but it makes a lot of difference for storage. *Wood Duck* also had an inboard engine, and I had long since learned that although an outboard hanging over the stern was all very well from a servicing point of view (if there were problems I merely lifted it off and took it to the repair shop), if I tried to motor along in any sort of wave conditions, the propeller sometimes lifted right out of the water, revving up the motor speed and almost stalling when the propeller struck the water again, thereby endangering the shaft. The older wooden boat was possibly more fragile than my fibreglass San Juan, but Paul worked hard maintaining *Wood Duck*, and he knew most of its foibles.

I assumed that the boat, with its heart-shaped transom, was a Herreshoff, but Nichol Warn of Sechelt, who has studied and built sailboats for years, assures me that it was probably a home design by a knowledgeable person. Brahm, who built *Wood Duck*, lived and worked in Idaho, but little else is known about him. According to both Warn and Neil S. Thompson (another boat wizard), the hull is much like those produced by Walter McInnis of the Eldridge McInnis Yard in Boston. McInnis's boats, with their sweet sheerline and slightly elevated bow, were ideally suited to the short, choppy waves commonly found in Massachusetts' Buzzards Bay and in British Columbia's Strait of Georgia. *Wood Duck*'s hull was deep, with a cement-enclosed keel. It drew five and a half feet when loaded, weighing in at approximately 8,000 pounds. The planking was one-and-a-quarter-inch yellow cedar on bent oak frames. The fact that the deadwood was not planked hints

Wood Duck is pictured here on the grid at Cortes Island, where it stayed while its bottom paint dried.

at a home design, but with an 8-foot beam for a 26.5-foot hull and a 41-foot 9-inch mast, *Wood Duck* sailed like a happy witch.

Wood Duck, like my *Saffron*, was designed to serve midgets only. There was simply no headroom. The advantage of this arrangement was that the power of the sails was as close to the surface of the water as possible, but it took some patience when you moved around inside, and you cooked or did the dishes while kneeling in an attitude of prayer. The bronze deck fittings were all the originals, which made my heart sing. No more peeling chrome, just a nice greenish patina. The cabin top was sealed with stretched and painted canvas, like my father's old boat, the *Loumar*. Where the cabin joined the deck there were rainy-day leaks in mysterious places, but they stopped when the wood became swollen. As far as I was concerned, it felt like home.

Paul had found *Wood Duck* in Seattle in 1971. It was a tired-looking mess, and the engine, a 25-horsepower Kermath, was all in pieces on the dock. The boat belonged to a Korean war vet who had bought it so that he could take his homesick Korean wife back to see her parents. The boat had no water tank and carried only fifteen gallons of gas. Apparently they got as far as Cape Flattery, where a storm and a balky engine forced them to return to Seattle. The vet decided to sell the boat.

At the time, Paul was teaching at Vananda, near Powell River. During his summer holidays he was helping his friends Warren and Ginny Tormey resurrect an old homestead on the southeast corner of Cortes Island, and he needed some sort of boat to get himself there and then back to his job. This little sailboat appealed to his sense of adventure and his frugality. The wind was free. Why not use it?

Paul bought the boat, threw all the small engine bits into the trunk of his car, lugged the engine block up to the storage shed to be picked up on a future trip and drove home to Vananda, three ferry rides away. When he wasn't busy with schoolwork, he cleaned the parts, guessing what fit where and organizing all the sub-assemblies. Two weeks later he drove back and put together what he could of the engine. The water pump shaft and its seals were badly worn, with water pouring out of the connection, so he took everything back to Vananda and machined a new stainless steel shaft from an outboard engine part. Paul loved working with metal and thrilled at the creative challenge of taking a scrap of material and producing a thing of function and beauty. Being a tool-and-die maker by trade came in handy.

After assembling the engine and borrowing a battery, he gave it a crank and it started, but ran very roughly. He tuned the ignition, adjusted the carburetor, and the engine began idling quietly, drifting a plume of smoke gently out the door of the shop. He later told me he never regretted the experience of getting to know his engine so intimately.

As a small marine gas engine, the Kermath was hard to beat. This particular model was called a Sea Cub and boasted a reverse gear. For many years marine engines had not come so equipped, and the unlucky owner had to stop the engine and restart it by cranking it in the reverse direction if he wanted to avoid a collision. Muriel Wylie Blanchet, who wrote the classic *The Curve of Time*, had a Kermath in her little ship *Caprice*. Like Paul, she learned to disassemble it so that she could do her own emergency work should it let her down. She travelled the BC coast with her five children and a dog in a small wooden boat in the 1920s, before the advent of cellphones, rescue craft and assorted marine services that baby us today.

Getting the engine installed and running was only the beginning of Paul's battle. He still had to get his sailboat home. It was just as well that he had gained some boating experience while he lived near San Francisco. In the 1940s he went along for a few training sessions on a 48-foot ketch and enjoyed a few afternoon outings on a small day-sailor, so the principle of using the power of the wind was not entirely foreign.

With this modest amount of knowledge, he purchased a book of charts and planned his trip home to Vananda. After getting help taking his boat through the locks at Seattle, he put in a hard day's sailing and got as far as Port Townsend on the Olympic Peninsula. Then the weather turned sour. Storm-warning flags streamed from the signal pole for three days before he was able to set out again. He arrived, exhausted but jubilant, at Friday Harbor after a riotous sail that tested him to the utmost. Weather reports continued to be pessimistic, and the Easter week holidays were rapidly drawing to a close, so he elected to leave the boat at Blaine on the American side of the border because he still had to deal with customs officials about taking it into Canada.

A month passed before he and a young teaching pal hitched a ride to Blaine so they could make the long passage back to Powell River, a port of entry. They could not legally stop anywhere en route. Paul said that snow was blowing and the tops of all the mountains were hidden in white as the boat ran before the southeaster that drove them all the way past Point Roberts, along the length of the Strait of Georgia, past Thormanby Island and alongside the coast of Texada Island to Powell River, where a simple phone call to the official completed the transaction.

He moored his treasure at the little Vananda Yacht Club dock near his work, where he could spend evenings and weekends adapting it to his needs.

2 OUR ADVENTURES BEGIN

For the first nine years with *Wood Duck*, Paul spent his summers helping Warren and Ginny Tormey on Cortes, with the odd morning spent fishing. Now and then they made a run up to Big Bay on Stuart Island, where John Wayne also loved to fish, but most of the time they were deeply involved in projects around the Tormeys' homestead.

On his annual trips from Richmond (where he now lived) up the coast to Cortes, the idea of going farther always floated through his mind like a will o' the wisp. But his strong work ethic kept him from throwing caution to the wind and continuing north. As well, the lack of a skilled companion slowly pushed the dream into the corners of his mind.

My arrival on the scene changed all that. In 1976, three years before I met Paul, I bought a little mustard-coloured, 24-foot San Juan sloop, aptly named *Saffron*. Although I knew little about sailing, I took my young son as crew and we bumbled up the coast as far as Cortes Island. As the years passed, I gained experience and began racing *Saffron* with the first all-woman crew in BC. Summers were spent exploring the lower coast. (These experiences are documented in my second book, *Shelter from the Storm*.) One year I mustered up the courage to venture all the way to Knight Inlet with Eleanor Frisk, one of my racing crew members. The heady experience of travelling past the various rapids on our way had me vowing to return another summer and continue even farther north.

In those years I also acquired chart work and sailing experience that Paul lacked. We both had a sense of adventure that involved poking into unfamiliar waterways and anchoring in quiet bays with endless shorelines to explore on foot. The fact that I was a devoted fisherman was icing on the cake. So our adventures began.

In 1980 I left *Saffron* in Vancouver for my crew to use, we loaded Paul's boat with supplies, including a shopping bag of my charts for the waters between Cortes and the middle coast around the Knight Inlet area, and away we went. The trip was a delight because I was totally confident in retracing the path I had taken before. We revelled in the good crabbing and fishing in the waters around Minstrel Island in Knight Inlet and revisited Mamalilaculla, where Eleanor and I had discovered the ocean was pure glacial freeze.

I shared with Paul the wonders of the place. We explored Grave Island, photographed the derelict fishing boats marooned along the beach, marvelled at the longhouse support posts and the few handsome carved totems that still existed in this deserted Native village. Of those that had managed to survive the ravages of time and theft by White people intent on selling them to museums, the handsome, enigmatic face on top of the short bear totem had become my favourite. This mortuary pole leaned among seedling apple trees behind a small cottage and was soon to fall back and rot into the soil from whence it came.

Near the house we found raspberries begging to be picked. After a few minutes of exclamations and happy nibbling, we were startled from our feast by an odd-looking, stocky woman who came plunging through the bushes clutching a rifle. She was dressed in ill-fitting men's clothing and had an old hat jammed on her unruly hair. Glaring at us through the smoke rising from the hand-rolled cigarette that dangled from her lower lip, she snarled, "Don't you idiots know there's bears around here?" With all our chatter about the plump berries we had been scarfing, I doubt the bears were anywhere within five miles, but that didn't deter Annie-Get-Your-Gun from lurching away, looking for something to shoot. Following hot on her heels was an even shorter husband.

Paul and I looked at each other and then doubled up in silent laughter. Had we dreamed that apparition or was she real? We found out later that evening.

We had anchored in the small bay near an old dock. While we were lounging on the back deck, enjoying the afterglow of a perfect day, Paul spotted a black bear and two cubs on the beach. Mama set to work turning over stones, looking for edible treasures, but the young cubs had different priorities. One after the other they clambered up a cedar tree that overhung the ocean, wrapped their paws around a branch and slid down rump first to land with a splash in the shallow water. Then they chased each other back to the tree to repeat the performance. Their squeals of delight brought chuckles to our throats.

Then a shot rang out! We turned to look in horror at the old East Coast cod-fishing boat that was anchored nearby, and there was "Annie" on the back deck, raising her gun to let loose another volley. In the encroaching darkness, her aim was off and all three bears scrambled into the brush, apparently unharmed. I stood up and was about to shout in protest, but Paul laid a hand on my arm to restrain me. "June, she's got a gun and her dander is up. Just be quiet." We considered alerting the Coast Guard to the presence of this menace, but figured she likely monitored the airwaves. Our boat had a thin wooden hull, so we were no match for a gun-wielding zealot. It was a relief to wake up in the morning to an empty harbour.

In 1981, this mortuary pole at Mamalilaculla had weathered the ravages of time and theft. It has now fallen and rotten away.

Now we needed to do some serious fishing. Without refrigeration, chasing protein was an almost daily task—not a hardship, although it did take time. We sampled just about everything the sea had to offer, from fish to clams and even snails, but salmon remained our favorite. If the fish we caught was bigger than we could eat in two days, we preserved the excess in jars using my small pressure cooker. In time we learned to pickle it, just like herring. But our favourite meal was smoked salmon. This proved to be a challenge when we had neither an electric smoker nor a land-based smokehouse.

After leaving Mamalilaculla, we trolled our way back toward Minstrel Island, where I managed to hook an 18.5-pound red spring salmon. We couldn't eat all of that in two days and I didn't want to spend hours canning the leftovers, so we decided to improvise a smoker. We anchored in nearby Potts Lagoon, cleaned and gutted the salmon and put the offal in a crab trap. Then we sat on the back deck, sipped a late-morning cup of coffee and tried to decide what to do.

Certainly the first task was to apply pickling salt along with brown sugar to draw out the moisture. That was easily done in a plastic tub right on the back deck. But how were we to cut up the fish—in strips or rectangles? Paul came up with the idea of suspending whole fillets on a series of fishing hooks tied to a line. The hooks would pierce the skin so that the fillets could be hung perpendicularly over the incoming smoke.

If we had known at the time how the Native people did it, we would likely have woven the flesh onto cedar sticks and mounted them in a circle around a beach fire. And years later my cousin Rod told me that we could have formed a teepee out of bark peeled off an old dead cedar tree and used sticks to support the pieces of fish, but we were total beginners. Our mental picture of smokers was that they were like little houses, with the fish supported on racks through which the smoke passed as it rose from the fire.

Based on this assumption, we set out to devise a smokehouse. Paul took his hunting knife and small hatchet ashore and prepared four long, forked sticks. He made cross braces to steady the top, and I found a sheet of heavy clear plastic washed up on the beach. This was our homemade smoker. We had a little iron hibachi, and we reasoned that if we built a fire in this and somehow directed the smoke into the bottom of the unit, we could smoke the fish very nicely.

In the morning, Paul took on the task of attending the smoker on the beach, a 10-hour chore. He got a nice fire going in the hibachi, then fed it with green alder chips to produce an aromatic smoke that would slowly cook and flavour the meat. Meanwhile, I struggled on the back deck with the many huge crabs that had obligingly crawled into our trap overnight. I cooked, shucked and canned crab in tiny quarter-pint jars, making numerous trips ashore to see how Paul was doing. He had a pair of walkie-talkies, so he took one with him and I was supposed to call him regularly. I had never used one of these beasts before and was already in the process of losing my hearing, so for all intents and purposes he was alone on the beach. The rowboat was with me. It was not until

Paul devised a smokehouse by preparing four long, forked sticks, securing them with a cross brace and wrapping them with clear heavy plastic. He then built a fire in the hibachi and directed the smoke into the bottom of this creation. Huge salmon fillets wait in the foreground.

evening that I realized how isolated he would have been had a black bear decided to respond to his smoke signals.

Paul reported later that when the fish was nearly done, the weight of the meat pulled the hooks loose, and the lot fell onto the gravel. He valiantly picked off the pebbles and bark chips, rinsed the fish with salt water and carried on with the task. A sampling had told him that it was almost done, so the final bit of smoking was more for sterilization than anything else.

The next big fish that we caught was smoked more elegantly. This time we had wire cake-cooling racks, strands of stiff metal and two cardboard boxes. When Paul hooked a 20-pound beauty in Retreat Passage, we simply powered up, went to Echo Bay for water and fuel, then moved down the inlet to a cluster of small islets near what is known as the Fox Group. We decided it would be smart to do our prolonged smoking away from bear country, so we chose a treeless rock, and both of us got to work. Paul rowed to the nearby shore to cut green alder branches while I prepared the salmon. It had already gone through the salting process. Now I had to rinse it and lay it out on newspapers to air dry. This forms a skin on the meat and prevents moisture from oozing out.

Paul set up the hibachi on a flat spot at the bottom of a little rock gully. Heavy tinfoil formed a collecting chamber over the fire, and the smoke travelled along a pipe made from milk cartons saved for the occasion. These were nestled in rocks to lead the smoke up into the cardboard boxes, which held the fish and were tied together with a generous lashing of duct tape. It had all the appearance and charm of a Rube Goldberg setup.

That evening we sat out on the back deck, ate homemade Swedish rye bread that I had baked in the old pressure cooker, sipped cool wine and gorged on smoked salmon until the grease ran down our chins. Nothing beats a snug anchorage, great food and a good companion, with a cozy berth waiting to be enjoyed.

3 REPLACEMENT PARTS

Our journey back down the coast that first summer provided its own share of excitement. We had spent the night anchored securely by the Misty Isles in Port Harvey. Our plan was to get an early start so there would be time to fish around the nearby Broken Islands before we tackled Johnstone Strait. Currents and wind can make this waterway a nasty experience, and getting on our way quickly would let us beat the usual afternoon west wind, which was going to be in opposition to the afternoon outflow of current.

It was low slack when we put our two rods in the water with the usual hope of snagging another big salmon. No sooner had Paul yelped and reached for his wildly bending rod than mine was hit with equal force. Paul put his foot on the tiller to nose the boat into deeper water as each of us struggled with what appeared to be twin spring salmon. But what broke the surface after a long struggle were two huge ling cod. I do not know any uglier face than that of a ling. It seems to be all gaping mouth.

After landing these monsters, Paul could not resist trying again. Before long the cockpit floor was no longer visible. It was covered in ling. As I write this, I am filled with remorse at our zeal. Our trip much predated catch-and-release, and in the early 1980s, no one thought the bonanza would ever cease. Today you are not even allowed to land this species of fish because the stock is so badly depleted.

We stopped in at Port Neville with our haul and hiked up to see Ole and Lily Hansen at their farmhouse, offering them some of our cod in exchange for advice about what to do with the rest of the fish. Ole's people had come to Port Neville from Norway in the late 1800s to log the huge trees that grew in that valley. Enough people were involved in this activity that Ole's grandfather saw the need for a local store, so he built the two-storey squared-log structure that endures today. When we were there in the early 1980s, the post office was still operating in the old building, but the store was no longer open for business because the two small logging camps up the inlet brought in their own supplies. Ole motored to Kelsey Bay for groceries, and the Hansens kept a cow and chickens to serve their own needs. Ole still pumped fuel into boats that tied to the nearby government floats.

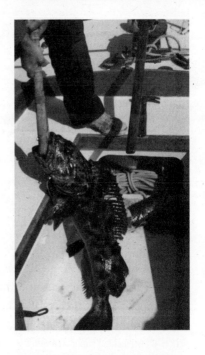

One of the ling cod we caught near the Broken Islands. Today we would not even be allowed to land one of these because the stock is so badly depleted.

We thoroughly enjoyed the warmth of their farm kitchen and Lily's shy smile along with the proffered cups of coffee. Ole quickly solved the problem of how to preserve our cod. Besides accepting our donation of fish, he gave us his grandmother's recipe for salting it down. He said that salt cod was a staple of Norwegians' winter diet.

As luck would have it, we had a new bag of coarse salt that we had purchased at Alert Bay. Besides that, all we needed were containers. There were three plastic tubs on our boat and one lidded ice-cream pail, and Lily found two more of these handy pails in her pantry. Ole said they would do just fine.

According to Ole's recipe, we had to mix enough strong brine to completely cover the fish when it was packed in the containers, with loose salt sprinkled between the layers of cod. He told us, "Now when I say a strong brine, I mean one that will float a potato. Not below the surface but right up on top. For the first few days you will be able to just scoop out a piece of fish and cook it as it is, but after the first week you will have to soak it in water to draw out the excess salt. By midwinter you will want to soak it all day. But the preserved cod will keep in a cool place for a long time. If the liquid gets stringy, you can pour it off, rinse the fish and add a fresh batch of brine."

We followed his instructions to the letter and he was right, but I have to admit that by early spring it was just about impossible to remove the excess saltiness. We began to appreciate the wonders of frozen fish as opposed to salt fish, and we began to understand what life was like in earlier days or, for that matter, in places like Portugal today, where this kind of food is still a mainstay of the national diet.

Luckily it was the end of our summer, and most of our supplies were running out, so there was room under the side bunks for the containers. Even so, we felt like squirrels with bulging cheeks as we set out on our way next morning.

As we putted along back to Cortes Island, we worked on our list of projects for the coming winter. One thing that had tried my patience that first summer was the quality of the headsail. It was altogether wrong for the boat. It turned out that it was a carry-over from when the rig was seven-eighths and the forestay reached only partway up the front of the mast. Now the forestay went right to the top of the mast, putting the sail at a steeper angle than was appropriate, so of course it worked poorly. I asked Paul why he had changed it, and he sent me to his logbook to read up on his dismasting.

This disaster occurred in 1977. As usual, he had put off the return trip to Richmond until the last minute. The skies were overcast and there was a small craft warning, but it didn't look too bad when he set out from Cortes, and there were places he could duck into for shelter along the way. At first the winds were on the beam because southeasters tend to be deflected by the mountains of lower Desolation Sound, but as he approached the Powell Islets the winds switched to head-on and increased in velocity to about 30 knots, becoming gusty. He raised the sails because he was no longer making headway with just the motor and he thought he could make some sort of progress tacking back and forth.

Suddenly a bigger gust hit and broke the mast in two places, bringing everything crashing down onto the deck and into the water alongside. The debris on the water acted like a sea anchor, causing the hull to swing off to leeward. Now the huge tangle of broken mast, sail and wires was all in the sea to windward and began slamming into the hull every time the boat lurched. *Wood Duck* began rolling dangerously from gunwale to gunwale, with the decks awash first on one side, then the other.

Paul's first thought was to radio for help from his friends back on Cortes, but he decided that it was far too rough for their little cruiser. His second thought was to try for the port of Lund, just past the Copeland Islands. But first he had to clear up the mess. After much effort he secured the boom alongside the hull with two sections of the mast. The lines, shrouds and sail were bunched in between the boom and the mast sections.

When he tried to start the engine, it failed, and he realized that the clutch was in reverse, but there was no problem when he put it in neutral. This told him that something was fouling the prop. He shut the motor down and set to work checking everything, then decided it must be the mainsail. With each roll of the boat, he managed to drag a bit more of the stiff cloth onboard, waited for it to drain, then hauled in a bit more, all the while fighting the pull of the ocean. He tied the sail off and turned his attention to one end of the broken mast, which lurked approximately three feet behind the stern of the boat and several feet below the water. Using the boat hook, he was able to tussle it closer and tie it off to the stern towing bit. Then he wrestled with the genoa and finally got it loose and stuffed into the cabin.

This time the engine started without complaint. He eased into forward gear and inched along in the direction of Lund, his awkward tow working up and down with each swell. When things seemed more settled, he thought to call his friend at Cortes but realized that with the coaxial cable nearly cut in two and with the radio-telephone antenna still attached to the mast, which was now deep underwater, he was completely alone.

He finally arrived at Lund, tied to the float and proceeded to dismantle the mast-supporting stays, freeing the mast and lifting the sections onboard. One piece went from the back of the cabin to about two feet in front of the bow, while the other fitted inboard of the stanchions on the other side of the deck. Strangely, the solid wood of the slim mast showed no signs of rot. After coiling the loose rigging and tying it to whatever was nearby, he motored out of the slop at Lund into Finn Bay, behind Sevilla Island, and tied to a small float for the night. He noted in his logbook that supper, when he finally got to it, was mighty tasty.

Next morning he headed for the port of Westview to take on fuel. On the way he noticed several small boats fishing near Hurtado Point. He slowed his speed to about half a knot and soon landed a six-pound salmon. After fuelling up in the nearby harbour, he started out again with the wind increasing and driving rain making life miserable at the helm. By the time he was past the shelter of Grief Point, the waves were flinging salt spray over the top of the cabin. Because he was taking it right on the bow, the hull speed dwindled to about two knots. Had he been able to set sail, it would have been a smoother ride. But by three in the afternoon the wind eased and the seas began to settle down. It was well past six o'clock before he anchored in quiet water at Pender Harbour. He noted in the logbook that supper was a delicious fresh salmon steak—a suitable feast for a tired sailor.

When he was back home, he called his insurance company to report his loss. The company promptly sent down a gorilla to inspect the boat. He tried to bully Paul into confessing that he had deliberately sabotaged his mast so he could get a new one. The upshot of all this hassle was not only a new mast, but also higher insurance rates, so he switched to another company. And along with the new mast, he decided to take the forestay right to the top of the mast.

Before we ventured north in 1981, my sailmaker, Gerry Storch, assessed the situation and recommended roller furling for the headsail. With roller furling, the sail is mechanically rolled up around the forestay, and you only pull out as much cloth as you need at any time. Gerry made up a new full-sized genoa to replace the little headsail and cut the boom shorter so that it would not hang up on the backstay during a tack. This necessitated a smaller mainsail, which was just as well given the area of cloth we were now exposing to the wind. The arrangement worked reasonably well, but now and then I found myself wishing that I could have handled the boat with the original sail plan. Tacking would be so much simpler with a smaller sail to pull around to the lee side of the mast.

With the new rig, we could sail if there was wind and could leave the motor just ticking over, with the genoa adding a bit of extra pull, when the wind weakened. This method allowed us to travel farther between fuelling stops. We would rarely need the jerry cans of extra gas.

Paul made several other modifications that winter. The least of these was a suitable chart rack. My grocery bag had long since overflowed with charts that were already suffering from too much repeated folding. New charts arrive rolled, so it was important that we decide how they were to be stored before any creases were made in their pristine smoothness. We decided that a shelf would fit nicely under the side deck above the skimpy side bunk. Now all our charts could be folded into foot-wide strips, labelled on the near edge for quick access. As navigator, I was responsible for buying any that we needed, so I refolded the old ones and tucked them away along with all the new ones. To make life easier, I kept the master chart on top and circled the numbers of those that we possessed. By keeping the pile in numerical order, I could get at any chart I needed with the least stress. This all sounds laughable in light of today's electronic mapping, but in those days we relied on the tough cloth-reinforced paper charts issued by the Canadian Hydrographic Service.

During the winter Paul also reinstalled the original wood stove, an antique twin-lidded beauty, narrow enough to fit inline with the sink. This project called for some major restructuring. First, he had to cut away a section of counter to make an alcove. To protect the wooden surroundings, he added zero-clearance insulation, using metal sheets with spacers to keep a draft of cooling air circulating between the hot stove and the wood nearby. The finished project looked classy and deflected the heat well, so the boat was safe even when the fire was burning merrily, keeping us dry and warm. It is so much cooler north of Cape Caution that, even on the hottest days, we rarely missed the little alcohol stove we used our first year.

While Paul was working on this project, I had the brilliant idea of putting a smoker box right on top of the cabin. There was just enough room for it inside the handrail aft of the smokestack.

Paul holds a crab claw above the tiny wood stove he reinstalled, which, thanks to his handiwork, deflected the heat well enough that the boat was safe even when a fire was burning merrily.

It occurred to me that we could introduce a diversion into the chimney that would lead the smoke aft into a smoker once you put a damper in the top. Obviously this setup could not stay on the cabin top while we were sailing—the main boom would toss it into the saltchuck—so inventive Paul set to work designing a collapsible box that fit over an enamelled meat tray I had unearthed in my father-in-law's workshop. Now we could even smoke the salmon while we motored along. No more struggling with incoming tides or bears.

4 BEFORE CAUTION

We set out that second summer with a vastly modified boat and the intention to explore the unfamiliar waters past Cape Caution, now and then pausing to enjoy some of the treats we had missed the previous summer.

On our way north, we chanced upon a huge fleet of gillnet boats spread out across our path with their nets almost blocking the way. This was our first encounter with such a large fishery, and we slowed right down to figure out the best route through the maze. Each boat had a net strung out behind the hull. Large inflated orange balls marked either end of the net, joined by a string of little floats that appeared and disappeared along the length of the obstruction. Since most of the vessels were tied to their nets, we aimed for the boat itself until we could locate a gap.

Right in the thick of the maze we spotted a large pod of killer whales that had come cruising down through Blackney Passage on their way to Robson Bight. This, too, was a new experience for us, and our hair rose right on end. Shining black scimitars rose up out of the water on all sides of our small boat. Steam whooshed from blowholes as the whales grabbed another lungful of air before sliding below the surface.

The whales casually worked their way through the fleet as though they had done this a million times. I was sure the fishermen were going to have to haul in their nets but, no, they hardly seemed to notice. Apparently this kind of whale does not tangle with the mesh. No doubt they snacked on some of the sockeye salmon, but their main objective was to get through to the rubbing beaches along the Vancouver Island shore. No one completely understands this phenomenon, but apparently the whales come nearly every day to this same area and take turns diving and rubbing their sides against the stony bottom, much like cattle do with a handy fence post. I guess it just feels good to scratch that itch.

After filling our cameras with the wonders of that day, we motored the last few miles to Telegraph Cove, a tiny slit of a harbour almost fully enclosed by trees and a rocky point, with much of the water occupied by a boom of logs. We tied to the float just inside the entrance and sat on the back deck to admire the bay with its absolutely clear water. The current from the neighbouring strait swept under the float, causing the brown kelp fronds to swirl and wave through the brilliant rays of blue and green light while the silver bellies of herring flashed as they darted hither and yon chasing food scraps. Sea urchins, ochre-coloured spider crabs and a multitude of sea life made this place a viewer's paradise.

At Telegraph Cove, the old sawmill had become obsolete and was in the process of shutting down, but a road connecting the isolated village to the Island Highway created new employment opportunities when whale-watching began bringing in tourists.

Next morning we motored across to the village of Alert Bay on Cormorant Island. This curve of land faces the mouth of the Nimpkish River on Vancouver Island, where Native people dwelt and trapped salmon for eons. It was two White men who decided that a settlement was needed on Cormorant Island. In 1870 entrepreneurs Spencer and Huson saw that money could be made from a salmon saltery; salting was the method used to preserve fish before canning became common practice. They planned to ship the boxes of salted fish to Victoria, because the Hudson's Bay Company had well-established markets for salted salmon in its outposts as far away as San Francisco and the Hawaiian Islands.

The two men reasoned that they needed to be near the river's huge salmon runs but away from the existing village if they were going to get any steady work done during the two-month period of the harvest. Therefore, the two men decided to locate on the island. It was not only near the river, but also centrally located on the middle coast, en route for traffic going north or south, with a reasonably deep, wide, sheltered harbour.

I did not feel surrounded by spirits when we were at Alert Bay, as I often do at ancient villages on the coast. There was no built-in history, no bottomless pile of discarded clamshells and no songs echoing down the slope of time. But there is certainly recent history. It didn't take Spencer and Huson long to figure out that if they could get the Anglican Church to move its mission from Beaver Cove down to Alert Bay, it would help them attract and retain workers. They offered Reverend James Hall part of their island. In no time he built a sawmill and trained young Native men to operate it, the better to get people out of the big communal houses and into individual homes. I noticed in old photographs that the big longhouses built along the beachfront by the chiefs of nearby tribes were all planked with sawn lumber that had undoubtedly been produced by the labour of their grandsons. Reverend Hall also built a residential school where Native boys from most of the surrounding settlements were housed and taught the ways of White culture.

At the same time, the ways of Native society were discouraged. The local Indian agent, William Halliday, disapproved of the potlatch. At these huge gatherings, hosted by a chief, a speaker recounted the illustrious history of the tribe, visitors were fed generously, and prodigious quantities of gifts were given to those assembled. This usually left the chief in a state of penury, but another chief, who sought to give away even more gifts, would later return his generosity. Potlatches were a type of insurance policy against want and also served to maintain the oral history of each tribe. However, they also went against the grain for the White settlers, who could not understand such behaviour. Halliday used his position of influence as Indian agent to have the potlatch banned, depriving the Natives of one of their essential cultural tools. He also confiscated most of the ceremonial regalia, selling some to museums and shipping the rest to Ottawa. The chiefs were supposed to be paid for those possessions that were seized, but few of them ever received any money.

Had the White newcomers taken the time to study the Natives' culture, they would have found startling similarities to their own. Native elders exerted a powerful influence for good that persisted in spite of the great damage wrought by alcohol and new diseases. If a son behaved badly, his father was duty bound to make restitution. According to James Sewid, in his book *Guests Never Leave Hungry*, maintaining the family honour was paramount. With no written history, the potlatch gatherings were occasions to renew the stories and strengthen the ties between related groups. In a culture governed by precedent, losing the chance to renew these stories hastened social breakdown and shattered ancient traditions. The loss of slaves and the availability of the White people's goods helped to beggar tribal treasuries. But the *coup de grâce* to a social structure maintained by communal living came when White missionaries urged young people to live in separate houses and speak only in the English language, detaching them and their children from their elders.

By the time we arrived in 1981, houses stood on either side of the single road that followed the shoreline to a small graveyard where garishly repainted mortuary poles huddled behind a fence.

With inactive canneries, a laundromat, a small church, a clinic, assorted other structures and a taxi, Alert Bay seemed a sad place. West of the government dock, up a winding road, we could see the old residential school that was built to house children from all the mid-coast First Nations during the era when church and state were trying to erase the Native language and customs.

Among my reference books is one entitled *The History of Alert Bay*, written by Elizabeth Healey in 1958 to commemorate British Columbia's centennial. The little booklet has a wealth of information, mostly about the White settlement of the island, and includes a number of photographs recording the history of the area. One such photograph shows the May Queen and her smiling attendants, all White girls; in the background is a small Native girl looking downcast. Less than 50 years later, however, in 2003, the May Queen for Quadra Island was a beautiful girl from the Native settlement at Cape Mudge. The tide has finally begun to turn.

We left Alert Bay in the calm of the early morning and were motoring to Port McNeill when I noticed that the compass headings seemed to be inaccurate according to bearings on the chart. This would never do. We were heading into unknown territory where summer fogs are the norm, so we had to determine how out of kilter our compass was. Since compasses react to nearby metal and electrical fields, they are almost always incorrect to some extent, especially on a small boat where there is little room for changing placement. The solution is to determine the deviation and then make sure you do not move metal objects, like spare anchors, within three to six feet of the compass.

I chose not to tamper with the adjustment screws on the compass housing and instead went to work with the new charts, finding some permanent day markers, clear of obstructions, that we could use to test our compass. Paul marked the fore and aft axis of the boat by putting a band of coloured tape on the bow pulpit and lining it up with the edge of the hatch glide so he would know when the hull was properly aligned to our observation points. While he handled the helm and called out "mark" when we were in line with an observation point, I hunkered down in front of our compass to determine how far its reading deviated from the one indicated on the chart.

We had our work cut out for us. Most points of land were not useful for establishing compass error because the height of the tide changed the apparent position of the point. Sometimes we had to line up a blunt headland and a fixed marker on a rock. There certainly weren't enough of these in one place to give us the complete picture, but there were enough between Port Hardy and Bull Harbour to provide a rudimentary table.

Eventually we discovered that the compass was out 32 degrees on the most extreme differential. When a compass bearing should have read 180 degrees, ours read 148.

Beaver Harbour, just south of Port Hardy, had several day markers that would help us with our project, and we were curious to see a place with so much history. During the Second World War there were military gun emplacements on one of the Cattle Islands to protect the nearby airport from invasion. And back in 1848, this harbour had been the site of a Hudson's Bay Company fort and trading post. Fort Rupert soon attracted a permanent settlement of people of the Kwakiutl Nation.

We managed to mark in a few more sightings for the compass table before dropping the hook in about 20 feet of water beside the Cattle Islands. Paul routinely used a trip line when he anchored. This device consisted of a large white float through which he strung a 40-foot length of sinking line with a huge knot in the end. This line ran freely through the hole in the float and led directly down to the anchor, to which it was firmly tied at the crown. The only drawback was that we could only use it in water that was not much deeper than 35 feet, a limitation that would cause us no end of trouble later on.

A bit of a west wind began to kick up while we ate our lunch, but the fetch across the bay was short so we did not worry. We were soon in the dinghy and headed for a stroll onshore.

The sloping beach blazed white with discarded clamshells that spoke of many a Native feast. After exploring the flotsam at tideline, we ambled inland where there was no underbrush to impede our way. The ground beneath our feet was soft with old moss and evergreen needles, punctuated here and there by the ghostly glow of empty abalone shells left by otters. As we progressed deeper into the woods, I began to feel a presence, a vibration in the air. This awareness intensified until a prickling sensation up my spine and a feeling of impending doom made me grab Paul's hand and hurry us back to the rowboat. What we saw when we broke out of the trees set us both to running. Our sailboat had come adrift, and the wind was pushing it toward the reef that was well down the shore to our left.

We scrambled into the dinghy, and Paul rowed like one possessed. He leapt up onto the deck and hurried to start the motor. Then he went to lift the anchor, but it was so heavy that I ran forward to help him. When it broke the surface, we could see why it had dragged along the bottom of the ocean. There was not one fluke visible. Instead of metal, all we could see was a writhing mass of brown kelp. By the time we got the trip line on board and were able to move the boat forward, the reef was only 15 feet to leeward.

Kelp balled around the anchor so that no flukes were visible.

I returned to Cattle Island many times on my own little sailboat and had no trouble if I anchored farther from shore, but a much better spot was over by Peel Island in a little indentation along the southwest shore. No summertime westerly could bother you there. But on that first visit on Paul's boat, we lacked both knowledge and experience. With the wind picking up, we lost confidence in that bay as a place of shelter. It was time to head for Port Hardy and tie up to the dock for the night.

Travelling by sail is an inexpensive way to see the coast if you use the wind, which is free (although the sails aren't), and if you anchor out instead of using the various docks. Paul had a great aversion to spending money, so we rarely tied to a dock. Now and then it was necessary so we could load provisions and use the laundry and shower facilities. These were usually only available at commercial enterprises such as marinas and the occasional fish barge. Although the amenities at the latter were intended only for the fishermen, we were never turned away. Perhaps our humble wooden boat escaped notice. Or maybe the staff was too busy to care.

Provisioning usually meant fresh vegetables, fruit and baked goods. Paul's boat had no refrigeration, so we bought little in the way of fresh meat. Yes, we needed fruit, vegetables, eggs and a bit of bacon now and then, but Paul preferred homemade granola served with powdered milk. At that time there was a great mix of dried sweet red peppers available at health food stores. I stirred this into scrambled eggs, where the dried peppers softened and added flavor as well as a touch of colour. This just about eliminated the need for perishable bacon. I was from pioneer coastal stock, so in the winter I canned meat in short, wide bottles known as salmon flats. This provided us with jars of turkey thigh meat, roast beef, etc., and when these became empty, I refilled them with salmon.

We used much dried food, sprouted seeds for salads, took along durable veggies and fruit, and were both good fishermen and shore foragers, so there was little need for large shopping trips when we did hit the outports. We found that the chilly seawater north of Desolation Sound was a great help in keeping food cool. Anything that needed special care was placed on latticework that held it near the hull under the waterline but away from the occasional slop of water in the bilge. I found that if I wrapped newly caught fish in newspaper to absorb the slime, then packaged it loosely in plastic bags, it would keep for up to three days. And who wants fish that's more than three days old anyway?

I baked bread in an old pressure cooker. If I sat the round bread pan on three metal canning-jar rings to raise it a bit and really pre-heated the pot, I was able to make terrific seedy rye bread. At that time I was a devotee of one of the early vegetarian cookbooks, *Recipes for a Small Planet,* and found its Swedish Limpa bread to be a real winner. The aroma of this drifting downwind brought many a lonely fisherman rowing over to the boat to offer us a salmon fillet or a cooked crab. What better use for bread? When we ran out of baked goods, there was also frying-pan soda bread, scones or hardtack, so being away from stores was no real worry for us.

But, oh, how we revelled in the occasional shower. Away from port we did not squander our five gallons of drinking water on too much cleanliness. Salt water and mild detergent answered many of our needs. The ocean that kept our food cool also discouraged us from swimming, so when we felt grubby at sea, we hit the high spots with a washcloth and left it at that. It was enough to keep us still speaking to each other.

After our provisioning stop at Port Hardy, we cruised to Bull Harbour on Hope Island, nearly at the "top" end of Vancouver Island. We felt truly adventurous as we cruised up Goletas Channel, with the smooth shoreline of Vancouver Island on our left and numerous small islets on our right that kept us examining the charts and marvelling at the variety of bays and passageways that opened up into Queen Charlotte Strait. How much simpler this journey was for us than for the early Spanish and English explorers who ventured up these waterways. We had detailed charts with carefully marked soundings, whereas they were a long way from home and help.

When we finally arrived at the entrance to Bull Harbour, we paused to eye the notorious Nahwitti Bar just to the west. "Oh boy, look at those breakers," I said. "Let's not go that way when we head for Cape Caution." In the outer harbour we saw the sea lion caves that likely gave this place its name. Paul stopped the motor (mustn't waste fuel) and we got out our cameras, but the lighting was wrong so we decided to come back in the morning,

The motor refused to cooperate when Paul tried to start it. I soon had the sails up and set to work tacking our way into the anchorage while he muttered and mumbled down below. It is fortunate that all my years of sailboat racing had me trained for just such an occasion. A sculling oar would have been handy, but there was enough of a residual breeze to get the hull moving. I pumped the tiller occasionally, which is strictly illegal in racing but works well in everyday maneuvering. Every so often Paul stuck his head up and said, "Amazing," before going back to work to solve the problem. Before long I had the boat far enough into the harbour that we could drop the hook. We were obviously a good team for the adventures we were undertaking.

Within the bay were two fish-buying barges and what appeared to be a zillion fishboats either tied alongside the nearby dock or anchored helter-skelter everywhere. We were puzzled by the obvious lack of activity, but when we rowed over to the barge farthest into the bay, we got our answer. They were in mourning. A few days earlier, Bob Parton, the manager of the other barge, had been killed when he was sucked into the maw of the ice auger.

At the time of the tragedy, Bob and Pat Parton were on the BC Packers barge with their teenaged son, their pregnant daughter and her husband, Dave Allen. This family had run the barge as a summertime project for a number of years, delivering ice to the trollers, accepting their catch for transfer to the Lower Mainland, keeping them supplied with groceries and other necessities, and supplying showers and laundry facilities so that the fishermen lost no time between sessions out on the grounds.

Chipped ice was stored in a pair of adjoining rooms with the power control switch outside the entry door. At this time, these insulated storerooms were packed almost to the ceiling with slippery hills of ice waiting to be delivered into the holds of boats that tied alongside the barge when their turn came for loading. The ice is fed into a hopper with a large motor-driven auger at the bottom of the funnel. This auger consists of sharp metal blades that simply chew through loose material, much like an old-fashioned meat grinder, and send it down a wide, articulated, metal pipe.

A few days before Paul and I arrived at Bull Harbour, the refrigeration system on the barge had malfunctioned, and the ice, which should have been in flakes, had begun to melt and then had refrozen, forming lumps in the mix, while the cooling system was repaired. When a solid clump dropped into the hopper, the auger would sometimes jam, and the operator had to clear the jam in order to keep the ice flowing smoothly down into the waiting hold of the troller tied alongside the ice barge. A fisheries opening was coming up soon, so the fishermen were all anxiously waiting their turn to take on ice so they would be ready to leave for the fishing grounds on time. Government conservation efforts had cut more and more time off the season for these fellows, who nearly all faced big mortgage payments on their boats and were anxious to get going. The barge operator would have felt a lot of pressure to keep the ice flowing quickly and smoothly.

When the accident happened, Bob Parton was operating the auger, with his son-in-law nearby helping to shift ice. The proper procedure during a jam was to go outside the storerooms and shut down the machinery, but this time Bob tried to clear it while the unit was still under power. He may have slipped, although no one knows for sure. The next thing Dave heard was the awful scream when the blade caught Bob and began dragging him into the auger. The young man realized that by the time he struggled through two rooms packed ceiling-high with heaps of ice and got to the control switch outside the door, it would be far too late to save Bob, so he lunged toward him and tried to pull him loose. The immense power of the machinery dragged Bob relentlessly into the blade, pulling the son-in-law along with him and beginning to grind away on his arm, too. All that saved Dave's life was the fact that Bob's body finally jammed the mechanism and stalled the gears.

No wonder the whole harbour was quiet. People sat on the back decks of boats, talking quietly, nursing cups of coffee while cigarette smoke rose and drifted away in the still air.

In the afternoon we rowed to the beach so we could visit the Coast Guard station. The wireless communications room was in a small clapboard building facing the ocean. Two or three officers were on duty, and Paul nearly fainted when he saw the antiquated equipment they were struggling to maintain in spartan surroundings. He had a natural ability to get men talking about

When we arrived at Bull Harbour, we found a gathering of fishboats as people mourned the tragic death of the manager of a fish-buying barge.

their trade, so before long we were on our way to one of the residences to have a cup of tea with the officer and his wife. He was from the Maritimes, had gone on holiday to Mexico, fallen in love with a local woman, married her and brought her and their little daughter to this chilly, fog-shrouded place. She was a brave lady and kept an immaculate house. It was one of several modest homes set back away from the beach and, I hoped, away from the worst of the winter winds. A long skinny line of floats stretched out from the beach toward the bay, but as it was low tide the sections were just sitting in the mud. At high tide on a hot summer's afternoon you could likely have a swim in the shallow water.

After tea and a visit, we ended our afternoon by exploring the exposed side of the isthmus. Roller Bay is aptly named. The swaths of large round pebbles made walking on the high, sloping beach a challenge. They rolled and rattled beneath our feet as we struggled to move forward. With the constant surge of Pacific swells into this wide bay, it was easy to see how these stones have been tumbled and polished until they gleam like agates in the salty mist.

Since our visit, the Bull Harbour Coast Guard station has been closed, and if you wish to go ashore to enjoy that glorious beach you must pay a fee to the Natives who have reclaimed the land. Some members of the Nahwitti Band who had been living at Alert Bay came here shortly after the turn of the new century, renamed their band Tlatlasikwala and began living in the abandoned Coast Guard settlement. According to an article Mark Allan wrote for the *North Island Weekender* newspaper of November 29, 2003, the band now numbers about 55 persons, with some of them joining Chief Tom Wallace and his family during the summer. No doubt they have had a few heated discussions with the kayakers who had begun to view the deserted cabins as their own.

Bull Harbour ranks right up there with other dreadful lapses in judgement regarding treatment of the Aboriginal people on this coast. The relationship between the nearby Nahwitti tribe and the Hudson's Bay Company was never good. For one thing, this tribe had been severely debauched by whiskey traders who prowled this coast before the HBC fort was established. The Nahwitti men became aggressive when they were drunk. But some of the problems were the result of Chief Factor William McNeill's autocratic manner in his dealings with the Natives, and also with company employees and the Scottish miners who were under contract to extract coal from the area.

According to T.W. Paterson in his book *Vancouver Island*, two HBC seamen deserted their ship when they learned of the California gold strike. They intended to stow away on another boat leaving Fort Rupert, but when the company ship, the *Beaver*, hove into sight, they vanished into the woods instead. Under the rules of the day, desertion was an act punishable in the most severe manner, so their decision to run for cover was understandable. They had been warned that the Nahwitti were a fighting bunch, so when they met a group of braves, the seamen swore at them, threw rocks, slashed the air with their knives and generally behaved aggressively. In response, the Natives killed them.

During negotiations with Dr. Helmcken, who was the company doctor and also the local magistrate, the Nahwitti chief offered reparations for the killings, as was customary for his people, but refused to hand over his men. The chief's argument was that the deserters had acted so dreadfully they deserved to be killed.

Neither side was willing to give way. Finally, Richard Blanshard, governor of the colony of Vancouver Island, ordered the crew of HMS *Daedalus* to storm the village. When these sailors discovered that the Natives had disappeared, they burned the village. The Nahwitti retreated to Bull Harbour and fortified their encampment, only to have it and 20 canoes totally demolished by the cannons of two warships. The Nahwitti never quite recovered from the onslaught.

During our visit, the only Natives around were the few who were part of the commercial salmon fishing fleet. We did, however, motor down to the lower end of Hope Island to see the abandoned Nahwitti village site at Kalect Island. What a precious spot to call home! Although the houses have long since disappeared, one can appreciate the beauty and sense of security that drew people here in the first place. The view in all directions was superb, with the village site on a flat point of land facing the sun. There was also shelter nearby where fishing boats could anchor in a niche between the islet and the shore. We spent a few hours adding to our supply of compass corrections, using local day markers as reference points. Then we anchored near the deserted village for the night.

We harvested our first huge sea urchin here. As we rowed alongside a steep bluff, we saw the urchins in all their purple glory about three feet below the surface of the water, moving over the rock face as they harvested the soft growth to be found there. They were covered with spiny quills that moved like so many little legs. Sea urchins are related to starfish and have a similarly positioned mouth, centred underneath the body as it moves over the grazing meadow.

I had been experimenting with Japanese cuisine, particularly a dish called sushi that was starting to appear in Vancouver specialty restaurants. Up to now we had only eaten sushi rice decorated with strips of salmon, either raw or smoked. I also had a few tins of smoked eel, but sea urchin roe was something we had only sampled at sushi bars, not out on the water. We were pleasantly surprised to find that the fresh roe we harvested had an exquisitely delicate flavour. Each piece looked like a section of pale mandarin orange and was almost as firm. We had to break up the shell to get at the roe because the segments were nestled shoulder to shoulder inside their protective covering. I cooked the sticky rice, cooled it, added the correct seasoning, formed it into small oval balls and tucked rice and roe inside a collar formed of nori (dried sheets of seaweed). We dipped these morsels into soy sauce served in the bowl of an oyster shell. A small jug of sake, warmed in a pot of water on top of the stove, helped us feel very Asian indeed.

5 BEYOND CAUTION

On the morning we planned to cross from the shelter of Vancouver Island to Smith Inlet on the central mainland coast, we awoke to find ourselves wrapped in fog. Even from the comfort of our warm bunk we could hear the horn at Pine Island moaning to ships at sea.

This was the day we would test our new deviation table as we crossed the exposed waters at the open end of Queen Charlotte Strait. To our port (left) side would be the Pacific Ocean; to our starboard (right), a scattering of the many tiny islets that clog the entry to the waterways on the inner side of Vancouver Island. But I did not feel sufficiently confident in our new tables to plot a safe course in the fog, when any significant wandering to starboard would put us amongst the rocky outcroppings. So we ate a leisurely breakfast and decided to move to the outer corner of Hope Island, near Roller Reef, where we could have an unobstructed view of our route.

Paul stayed on board because we didn't know how well our anchor would hold on the rocky bottom, given the current that was running past us. But I could not resist a walk on the beach, so I rowed ashore to look for glass fishing floats from Japan. These balls sometimes take as long as seven years to cross the Pacific Ocean. I did not find any of those treasures, but did find shampoo bottles bearing Asian script. It would seem that the Orient has its share of litterlouts. Nestled beside a huge rock was an empty brown Suntory whiskey bottle, its salt-corroded cap festooned with gooseneck barnacles that had come along for the ride. (It sits on my window ledge and stirs memories for me each time I try to dust it.) Just as I was about to climb back into the dinghy, I found a small plastic container with a long, narrow spout and an intriguing English translation stating that the contents were "Organ Oil." Hmmm, what sort of organ did they have in mind? I chuckled, tossed it in the dinghy and carried it back to show Paul.

We lingered until almost noon, when the fog lifted enough for us to see Pine Island and the lighthouse that had been calling to us through the mist. This raised our spirits, so we ate a hasty lunch. I had set a course, using our newly created table, which required that I add 32 degrees to the heading indicated on the chart. That's a lot of correction, given that there are only 360 degrees to a compass rose. Following John Chappell's suggestion in his book *Cruising Beyond Desolation Sound*, I allowed for current drift and the leeway caused by the Pacific swells that push you ever eastward, so the final correction was not quite as drastic.

After a few hours of motoring along on our course, we met the fog that obligingly returned to test our mettle. But we were able to set sail in the breeze that also arrived from the west. The huge ocean swells added to our feelings of adventure, and with the lack of visibility, we felt a bit like Columbus's crew expecting at any moment to fall off the edge of the world.

When we finally came within range of Egg Island lighthouse, just off Cape Caution, I found that we were considerably left of where I expected to be—we nearly sailed right past the island in the thinning fog—so I had subtracted too much off the heading to allow for the expected drift. This threw me. Where did the error lie? Had I relied too much on the cruising guide and abdicated my own responsibility?

There was no time to fuss about this error, because we were rapidly closing in on our destination. We furled the sails and motored between Egg Island and the North Iron Rocks. These rocks were boiling with the huge seas that washed over them. Fishermen call rocks like these "breakers" and rely on them for navigation. Seeing the effect of Pacific swells on these menaces gave me some confidence for future navigation. In the area I had come from, seas were often quiet, and underwater rocks remained hidden until I crunched into them or spotted the kelp beds that surrounded them. Now we had the almost constant swells to give us guidance through dangerous waters. With vigilance, we could either see or hear where rocks were located.

If we had been travelling this route 20 years later, we would have used a Global Positioning System (GPS) receiver, a satellite-guided device that would indicate our exact location. When this device is connected to a computer screen, you can see a chart of the area in which you are travelling. It shows your boat moving over the surface of the earth, and when you enlarge the image, you are able to pinpoint hazards. If you hook it up to your radar, you can also see other boats. But if your electrical system goes down, you become, as we were, totally dependent on your own senses.

Just as we drew clear of Egg Island, Paul noticed that the generator was no longer producing electricity, so it was just as well I was relying on my brains rather than some electrical magician. Even so, if we lost power in our battery, we would be totally isolated because our radio telephone and our echo sounder relied on that heavy black box. We wouldn't have been able to start the motor, either, but we could still have sailed and used our lead line to determine the depth of the water. (I believe that sailors are relatively safe on this coast provided they know how to use every breath of air and they deploy their anchors when the current overcomes the power of the wind. The ideal boat is one that is small enough to move by oar.)

Since our engine was still happily purring along, burning its usual excess of oil, we were able to work our way carefully through the last five miles that brought us to Jones Cove, the first available shelter past Cape Caution. It was after nine o'clock before the anchor was set, the fire was lit and the hot rums were in hand. We were glad to be safe in such a snug, tree-fringed slit of a harbour.

We woke to the realization that we had no fresh protein in our larder. We had been so intent on our goal of passing Cape

Caution that we had not paused to fish, so we set out to remedy the situation. The early morning light sparkled off the foam-washed rocks and shoals that spattered the mouth of Smith Sound, but the passageway inland looked like a good bet. In no time we hooked a small pink salmon—not the choicest of fish, because it does not keep well. We kept hoping that a spring salmon would take our lures, but after we caught four more pinks, we realized we were in the midst of a spawning run of that species.

Paul wanted to do more work on the cranky generator, so we returned to the familiarity of Jones Cove, where I set to work canning most of the salmon in the pressure cooker atop the tiny wood stove. The aroma of escaping steam from the cooking salmon stirred long-forgotten memories of my 17th summer in 1947, which I had spent working at Goose Bay cannery in Rivers Inlet along with three of my high school friends. When the huge retorts were opened, the steam rose up into the loft where the four of us worked, so we couldn't escape the permeating aroma. In those days, the cans were shipped flat with no bottoms. Our job was to run the equipment that shaped the cans, applied the bottoms and sent them on the conveyor to the lower floor, where the cut-up salmon was loaded, the tops were fastened on and the cans went into the huge pressure-cooking retorts on a wheeled rack. It was my first adventure away from home, and I returned with enough money to pay my university fees and buy my textbooks and even some clothing ($360 went a long way in those days!). I knew that the local canneries were no longer active, but I thought it would be great to see the place after all these years and find out if anything remained.

Paul agreed that the site of my youthful adventure in the next inlet deserved a visit, and we decided to set out right after breakfast, but when he tried to lift the anchor, it refused to budge. We both heaved on it, to no avail. Then Paul grabbed the boat hook, snared the trip line, wound it around the mast winch and cranked mightily. The boat heeled over under the strain and there was a sudden lurch, but we were still caught. After struggling for about half an hour, Paul paused for breath. We peered over the side and could see nothing

Our dinghy floats on the still waters of Smith Inlet on the central mainland coast, the morning after our foggy crossing from Vancouver Island.

through the murky water. As the silt gradually washed away, we saw that the anchor had broken free but the trip line was still wrapped around a log that was sticking up at a 45-degree angle from the bottom. While I released the strain on the line, Paul put the engine into reverse, and suddenly we were free.

This experience stopped my occasional grumbles about the bother of the trip line and the need to ensure it did not become fouled in the propeller. Without this safety feature, we might have lost our main anchor. Then we would have had to go directly upcoast to the supply depot at Namu to buy a replacement.

We emerged from the cove into a brisk northwest wind, just right for sailing. I was not mentally ready to try tacking through the maze of "breakers" that marked the many rocks encumbering the mouth of Smith Sound, so we made a beeline to port, out past Table Island, changed course and enjoyed a vigorous sail to the mouth of Rivers Inlet. The right-hand entry to this island-choked waterway was guarded by a rocky, tree-studded low point with intriguing beaches on the outer side and in the sheltered water behind. We elected to go inside the point, drop our hook, get in the dinghy and explore both sandy shores. Our stove had a continual hunger for bark and knots, so we combined treasure hunting with wood gathering.

Except for the firewood, there was nothing of note on the beaches, and we soon discovered why. The entire waterway inside the inlet was peppered with sport fishing boats. They were either rocking gently in the water with rods bobbing up and down or buzzing off to find a better spot. According to the logos painted on the hulls, they were from several different sport-fishing lodges, so the competition was fierce. I could only guess that they took an occasional break and went ashore to "stretch their legs," just as we had done. Like us, they would have checked out the tide line for treasures to carry home.

It was after seven in the evening when we finally approached my old workplace at Goose Bay. The signs advertised that it was a fishing lodge, but there was no one around and no floats as I had known them. I knew there had been pilings, so I was reluctant to pick out an anchoring spot in the area in case stubs remained underwater. I could not recall if the mud-bottomed bay past the old cannery site, by the mouth of the large stream that served the camp, contained any hazards, and I didn't trust Paul's primitive echo sounder to find us a safe spot. When we grudgingly turned back down the inlet, we saw a float and primitive cabin in a niche along the left-hand shore. We decided to tie up there for the night and row over to the cannery the next morning. A large, faded notice said *No Mooring Allowed* with an added note saying, "Tie-up fifty bucks an hour," or something equally ridiculous, but I was so tired by this time that I said, "Hey, it's late, let's stay here and see what happens."

Something did happen. Just as we were organizing a late dinner, a tough-looking hombre raced over from the cannery in an ugly metal skiff, paused about 20 feet away, waved a rifle in our direction and shouted over the roar of his oversized engine, "Can't you fuckin' read? That sign says no tie-up, so you had better either haul your asses outta here or pay up before I use my gun."

I tried to tell him that I had worked at the cannery and just wanted a visit in the morning. He got even more belligerent, so

Paul started up the motor while I jumped onto the rickety float to untie the lines.

When we were safely on our way, I burst into tears. The visit was important to me, but our reception had been so ugly that I couldn't believe I was still in Canada. Whoever heard of brandishing a gun to make a point? Paul patted me on the shoulder and said, "June, you can't go home again, no matter how much you might long for it. The past is gone, leave it there." He also mused that the hostile reception, and the seaplane we spotted near the cannery, probably meant there was a drug smuggling operation in the bay, and not a benign fishing lodge after all. Alerting the police via radio phone seemed a foolhardy venture, given the disposition of the caretaker. He would be monitoring the airwaves and knew this area a lot better than we did.

It was late in the day for finding a suitable anchorage, but I studied the chart in the failing light and located a bit of shelter. We wormed our way carefully into a shallow nook among some small islands, set the anchor, had something to eat and crawled gratefully into bed. No winds that got up during the night could have found us here, nor were we likely to be threatened by gangsters with weapons. In the warmth of the bunk, Paul wrapped his strong arms around me and stroked my hair. Some of the tension drained away, but it was a restless night, studded with fleeting dreams.

We set out next morning to explore the intricate passageways among the islands that choke the entrance to Rivers Inlet. Along the way we fished, as usual, with hopes of catching one of the large chinook salmon that make this a sport fisherman's Valhalla. No such luck. We caught three more pinks. When we anchored in Wilson Bay near an outfall to a lagoon, Paul went ashore to harvest firewood for the stove while I set to work canning. The black flies came to the party, so I hung gauze over the hatch and sweated away inside the cabin with one eye on the pressure gauge and the other on a book. Just as I lifted the cooker off the stove, I heard the rowboat tap the hull, followed by firewood tumbling onto the deck.

"Lots of good dry alder onshore," Paul said as he heaved more up out of the rowboat.

"Not a minute too soon," I replied. "This canning almost cleaned us out." We both dripped sweat, me from the heat in the cabin and Paul from sawing well-aged dry alder into chunks small enough to fit our tiny firebox.

Back on the boat, Paul set to work rearranging the stores in the lazarette to make room for all the new firewood. His disembodied voice echoed from under the side bench, "We're down to our last container of oil for the old Kermath. We better go looking for a supply pretty soon because I have to put this in the engine before we can start it again."

Next day, as we trolled around the Penrose Islands, we spotted a floating fish-buying camp in a narrow slit called Finn Bay. "Maybe they can sell us some oil," Paul said as he reeled in his line. We tidied up the cockpit and pulled in alongside the barge. "Can you spare us a can of oil and some water?" asked Paul.

"Not bloody likely," snarled the attendant. "We have no time for you sport fishing types. You're the reason the industry is dying. I can't deny you drinking water, but I'm sure not going to give you any oil." He handed Paul the black rubber hose that hung down into the ocean. It dribbled its way across the ragged deck of the barge as Paul led it back to our waiting tank.

We filled the tank, thanked the man and headed out of the bay. When I pumped some of the water into the kettle to make a cup of tea, I could smell diesel oil in it. Damn! It must have gotten onto the hose where it hung down beside the barge. A small spill from one of the old fishboats that came alongside the barge would be enough to flavour the water. Had we looked more carefully at the chart, we would have noticed Dawson's Landing just up the passageway. I don't know why the camp operator didn't tell us to go there instead of behaving so belligerently. We fished for food, but I suppose the two rods standing in the holders at the transom were enough to set him off on his rant.

We really needed that oil, so we set off up Fitz Hugh Sound en route to Namu. Later in the day we came upon scores of gillnet boats with their nets strung out in all directions, poised to intercept fish coming through Hakai Pass from the Pacific

Ocean. Some of these spawners were likely headed for the lake at Namu.

Like the fish, we were almost drooling at the thought of reaching that fabled place. For the fish it meant sex, at last! But for us it meant fresh food! A phone call home! Showers! Maybe even clean clothes! We had been away from civilization for 10 days. You could almost smell our boat as it wafted its way into the harbour.

At one time Namu was a huge BC Packers operation, much larger than the one at Goose Bay, with a cannery, dormitories, housing, stores, repair facilities and extensive docks. Canneries processed net-caught fish that were delivered intact, no gutting beforehand. This necessitated quick handling, so there were canneries just about everywhere. Seasonal staff was brought in to operate them.

However, the introduction of faster boats with refrigeration made upcoast fish-processing obsolete, and by the early 1980s, canneries such as this had become merely transfer sites. The catch was loaded into packers right in the fishing grounds. These packers, in turn, ran to places like Namu and off-loaded onto huge transport boats bound for the canneries at Steveston on the Fraser River or at Prince Rupert, farther north. This change meant that the companies no longer had to house and feed a huge staff onsite. The high-priced, troller-caught salmon for the fresh fish market were still sorted, weighed, iced and shipped from the plant onshore, but within a handful of years the stock of large chinook salmon was so depleted that trollers were limited to a few days each season. Gone were the days when people like my brother could fish nearly all year. We were witnessing the death of an industry and the way of life that went with it.

One of the key figures in the BC Packers family was the famous sailor John Newton, whose beautiful boat *Pachena* usually led the pack in races where I fumbled along behind with my tiny San Juan. Thanks to John's influence, cruising boats were welcome to tie up to the outer floats at Namu. Small gillnetters moored on the next two slips, where they could stretch out nets on the net racks for mending, while the huge seine boats mostly tied alongside the

At dusk, seine boats wait to unload salmon onto packers at Namu, once a bustling cannery located north of Port Hardy. The name means "place of high winds."

main wharf that led up to the marine ways at the repair shop. This facility was kept busy with everything from propeller replacements to patching damaged hulls. The machine shop next door hummed with activity.

As we walked along the boardwalk past the machine shop, we discovered the showers in a cement-floored building that had laundry tubs in the outer rooms and aged shower facilities at the back. I dove into the women's section, undressed in a little cubicle with a slatted floor and ran naked across to one of the shower stalls. The hot water sprayed from the overhead nozzle down onto my upturned face. Pure delight!

After my shower, when I had donned clean clothes from my backpack, the smell of my dirty clothes as I stuffed them into the bag reminded me that the next thing on my list was laundry. Since it seemed to rain a bit every day, I did not relish using the laundry tub in the women's shower room for the task, as the drying process would take forever. I knew there would be a laundry at the camp, and it was easy to find in a small building farther along the boardwalk. I confessed to the laundress that we were not fishermen, but she said she would try to do our load if possible.

Paul spent time with the cannery's electronics wizard while I shopped for provisions at the general store. It offered an impressive array of fresh fruit and vegetables, meat (mostly frozen), clothing, fishing gear, charts and a huge selection of liquor. Paul arrived in time to help lug everything back to the boat. Our washing was done, and we had learned that food was available to visitors at the commissary if we waited until the staff had finished eating. For seven bucks each, we had a choice of three entrees, veggies and dessert. No wonder people flocked to Namu.

After enjoying a great feast, we ambled over to the unloading bay, where trollers milled around waiting for their number to be called over a loudspeaker. These handsome fishing boats averaged 45 feet in length and had a look of success about them. We perched on the edge of the high pier to watch. The skipper climbed the metal ladder, stepped nimbly over the rim, paused to speak to a fellow with a clipboard, glanced at the sorting process and disappeared into the building. Meanwhile, a crane lowered a metal scoop right into the hold of a boat. You could peer over the edge of the dock and watch a worker forking huge spring salmon into the scoop. When the container was full, the crane hoisted it up and emptied the fish onto a stainless steel grading tray. Then down it went for another load. We drooled.

These were the elusive beauties that lured sport fisherman to this coast from all around the world. My brother, George, had spent his life chasing these silver treasures. When I asked him about his work he said, "What other job offers so much challenge, in such gorgeous surroundings? It is a life of great excitement interspersed with moments of hair-raising fear. People pay a fortune to do for a few days what I do all the time. This is where I belong."

Salmon practising their jumping skills dimpled the ocean beside the old cannery. It was time for us to see where they were going. We walked away from the unloading area, followed the boardwalk past a big entertainment hall and the "Namu Hilton" dormitories, and found our way up the hill to a wooden walkway that climbed beside the stream draining Namu Lake. We followed one determined fish as he made his way over the rocks against the current. He would rest for a moment in a small pool. Then, with a flurry of activity, he would make it past a section of fast water, only to pause again, gills pumping. When he slipped through a ray of light, his scales gleamed iridescent shades of green and blue, but in the shadows he was almost invisible. Sometimes he would be washed downstream, but he never gave up as he struggled to make it back to his birthplace. We cheered when he finally passed under the little bridge at the lakeshore.

The lake was right out of a travel brochure. Little white sandy beaches, cool clear water with evergreen trees touching down around the edges here and there, and a narrow footpath winding through the wild berry bushes that led you ever onward. I can see why loggers, like my handsome uncle Bill Illman in the 1920s, had come here on weekend holidays from Gildersleeve logging camp up Burke Channel. During the canning season, Namu, with its seasonal population of 2,000, would be flush with girls, the dance floor of the gymnasium would throb with lively music provided by a great Native band from Bella Bella, and there was always the lake for swimming. The salmon weren't the only ones seeking this beautiful spot to fulfill their dreams of hidden pleasures.

We had certainly fulfilled our dreams; we were clean, our tummies and the larder were crammed with food, and the fuel/lubricating oil problems were solved for the time being.

6 NEXT STOP: OCEAN FALLS

My parents had paused in Ocean Falls when they made their honeymoon trip by steamship from Vancouver to Dad's teaching job in Terrace in 1924. At that time, Ocean Falls was a veritable city, a seething mass of activity, all centred on the big paper mill. We had heard that it was now on the point of being dismantled because there was no longer a reliable supply of timber, and we wanted to see it before it disappeared.

Like most towns with a pulp and paper mill, this one had a weekend retreat away from the awesome smell for families who could afford it. We stumbled upon it by accident after enjoying a great 25-mile run under sail. The breeze that had pushed us along so obligingly died out just as we passed Benn Point, but it left us moving forward with just enough speed to make it into Wallace Bay and reach the shallows in front of a row of small cottages that were scattered along the shore like a handful of pebbles. Tree-clothed mountains rose sharply behind them, with their toes almost in the water. I felt that if the hills just shivered, the whole lot would be nudged into the deep. According to the chart, the mountain rose 900 feet in less than half a mile. The stream near the cabins must have roared in a downpour. But it would never match the noise in the town itself.

We set the anchor in the fan of mud near shore and sat back to admire this tiny enclave, the only sign of civilization for as far as the eye could see. Rays from the late afternoon sun glanced across the low valley on the opposite shore and brightened windows here and there among the cabins. Was anybody home? We felt like visitors caught in a time warp as we stepped ashore, but no one came to offer greetings or chase us with a gun. Trees sighed, a door creaked and mice scurried into the shadows. I strained to hear voices or perhaps a guitar or an accordion. But it was not the 1930s or '40s; it was now, and we were utterly alone.

The silence of Wallace Bay helped prepare us for the almost total abandonment that greeted us at Ocean Falls. There was a skeleton staff at the old hotel. The huge pulp mill that had belched steam, smoke and stench all those years was still. The sturdy houses, school, hospital and large docks were all quiet. We learned from a man at the hotel that a newer settlement along the shore near Martin River was still partially occupied.

As we climbed the plank roadway through the town, the eyes of empty houses followed us. But the only voice that met our ears came from the water burbling and sliding over the curved rock face as it drained down from the lake, past the mill and into the inlet. The trickle of water that flowed at the end of July barely wetted the surface. I felt a great urge to kneel down and stroke the exposed and convoluted granite shoulders that were worn silky smooth by eons of erosion. All was soothing now, but during winter rainstorms, the roar of the waterfall must have been deafening. When I read Paul Jones' book *Out of the Rain*, I learned that it rains just about every day there, so the ocean truly does fall.

Link Lake, at the top of the waterfall, stretches for miles, and the mountains that surround it would have provided huge quantities of timber for the voracious mill. You could see where the logs had been directed into the flume that carried them down to the pulp mill. How many discarded newspapers came from this vanished splendour? What stirring events had they reported? Vimy Ridge? VE Day? Pearl Harbor? The only news we got in that remote place was a radio telephone report of a float plane missing in the area. All mariners were asked to keep a sharp lookout for any signs of the plane, such as debris or oil slicks in the water. But we certainly couldn't see very far down the lake from the narrow elbow where we stood on the shore.

The little bay at our feet was to the left of the spillway. We looked out upon remnants of narrow docks and half-sunken boathouses. There were still a few small boats, but all looked neglected and forlorn. In my imagination I could see sailboat regattas, race committees and laughing groups of supporters. Surely the crowd of employees who worked in the mill and lived in the townsite included a few dedicated sailors. Or perhaps it was just my yearning for the thrill of the race that brought these visions to my mind. My friend Vern Logan lived in Ocean Falls for some years, and he said it would have been impossible to keep canvas sails from rotting in the constant wet. Anybody with any sense built a small boat, powered it with a one-cylinder engine such as an Easthope, and covered the lot with a top deck, so the little boathouses were a necessary feature in that remote and soggy town.

After visiting Ocean Falls we needed cheering up, so we meandered to Nascall Hot Springs, watching all the while for debris or oil slicks from the downed plane. At times like this one is almost afraid of what they might find. Along the way we paused to read the inscription on the rocky shore near Elcho Point that commemorates Sir Alexander Mackenzie's amazing pioneer journey across the continent. He got this far down what is now called Dean Channel and painted a simple notice on the rock— "Alex MacKenzie from Canada by land 22^{d} July 1793" (Canada being the early settlements nearer the east coast)—before turning back. According to my research, he was the first White person to cross the continent north of Mexico. It would be another 12 years before Lewis and Clark made the easier crossing farther south.

We Canadians do not know how to tootle our horn. I know more about Lewis and Clark than I do about the intrepid Scot who made this horrendously difficult journey with his cousin Alexander MacKay as his lieutenant, six French-Canadian voyageurs and two or three Natives in a 25-foot birchbark canoe. As a business partner in the North West Company, a fur-trading syndicate, Mackenzie ventured first into the Arctic on the river that now bears his name and "discovered" the Arctic Ocean. Then he returned to England to learn more about determining longitude before setting out two years later on his hazardous trip to the Pacific.

Mackenzie used the four moons of Jupiter to figure out where he was. It was the work of Galileo that provided the foundation for this rather laborious method. Galileo found that eclipses of these moons occurred 1,000 times in a year and were so regular that you could set your watch by them. Two hundred years passed before a dependable instrument, the sextant, and useful tables were developed for measuring both latitude and longitude by using the heavenly bodies. The celestial process required considerable mathematical skill. It was also important that the observer be standing on a firm surface, that there be no cloud cover that night, and that moon and earth were on the same side of the sun, a situation that existed for just two weeks each month.

Determining longitude required such ideal conditions that it took Mackenzie what seemed like an eternity to calculate his group's position in Dean Channel. This tried the nerves of his companions, as the local Natives were openly hostile to the White visitors, the result of an encounter earlier that summer. In an amazing coincidence, George Vancouver, captain of the *Discovery*, had been mapping the area two weeks before Mackenzie's arrival. According to the Natives, "Macubah" had fired on them when he came in his huge canoe, and another man, whom they called Bensins (likely Archibald Menzies, who was Vancouver's surgeon on the trip), had struck one of their members with the flat of his sword. Given that this particular group of Natives was acquisitive and appropriated just about anything of Mackenzie's that wasn't tied down, perhaps one can understand Vancouver's behaviour. According to the botanist Joseph Banks, Vancouver had a short fuse and never failed to lash out when he felt crossed, so his reaction was not out of character. What Vancouver did not recognize was that among the Natives, honour was everything. To be treated in this manner was an unforgivable offence.

As a result of what was seen as disrespectful treatment, these Natives had become so unfriendly that Mackenzie's crew threatened desertion if he did not turn back. They were afraid for their lives. They were also short of food but were fearful of going off alone to hunt or fish. A GPS device would have been a godsend to the embattled explorer trying to discover where exactly he was. (Come to think of it, I could have used one myself, given the fog we were to encounter later.) Luckily, the clouds cleared away enough for him to determine that they had reached 128.2 degrees west of Greenwich. That done, he mixed vermilion with melted grease, wrote his message on a rock and set out with his men to retrace their steps east.

While I decry the lack of public recognition of heroes such as Mackenzie, I am sad that nearby glories such as Nascall Hot Springs have become common knowledge. Before long someone will buy the property surrounding this treasure and "develop" it. When Paul and I arrived, however, we were alone. To the left of the hot spring, a stream flowed down through a broad, treed valley, ending in a grass-covered delta of the sort that attracts bears. The scalloped outer rim of this meadow was bordered by low mud banks reflecting mahogany brown and olive green onto the still water. There was no sign of habitation except for a humble shake cabin with a canvas door. (When I returned seven years later in my own boat, that little building was hidden behind a bunkhouse that had been dragged up over the beach to serve a small logging operation that was hard at work in the upper valley.)

There was no one around when we scrambled out of the dinghy and up over slippery rocks to peek inside. There we discovered two old claw-footed bathtubs with a raised walkway in between. Patches of rubber inner tube on cord provided stoppers for each tub, and two large black plastic hoses poured out glorious hot water from the spring in a continuous hearty stream. The excess went out the overflows and dribbled down around rocks through a velvety channel of viridian moss into the nearby ocean. Strangely, there was no apparent smell. But after a long soak, there was not a muscle left in our bodies. On rubber legs, we staggered back to the boat, ate a simple meal and fell into each other's arms in the forward bunk. Heavenly bliss!

Nascall was the farthest we would venture upcoast that year. August had arrived, so we made the loop from Dean into Burke Channel and began our homeward trip. The change in topography took our breath away. The upper end of Burke looked raw and new, with sheer rock faces, landslides, broken chunks of glaciers and fantastic rock forms. Sunlight sparkled off exposed minerals on steep cliffs. We decided that we just had to end the day early with a stop at Cathedral Point. Who could bypass a place with such a lofty name?

We passed through the entryway into what resembled a nave. Before us was a wall of rock formed into columns like the pipes of a gigantic organ. It seemed that at any minute, deep bass notes would begin vibrating the air, thudding sound waves against our chests. The satin floor spread to a low narrow beach on one side, with rocks to seat a phantom congregation. There was space for more pews on the opposite shore. A wide ledge that formed the right side of the opening looked almost like an artificial jetty— perhaps a place to dock your boat while you attended services? Solid rock rose perpendicularly out of the water and was almost flat on top. Here and there, old cables drooped down, festooned with bits of mooring lines.

Paul lay down to have a nap while I kneaded bread dough and kept the fire simmering. It was time to slow our pace and recharge our inner batteries. How I wish that I had taken along a sketchbook. But I sat out alone on the back deck while the bread rose, and I filled my eyes with the beauty of that place.

As the sun moved overhead, a late-day breeze began to ruffle the outer passageway. Streaks of cirrus began to form. By five o'clock it was apparent that we were in for a blow, but we were out of range of the weather station so could not check the forecast. Then the anchor began to skip and catch. At the rate we were shifting, we would soon be seated on the rocky pews ashore.

If we elected to lay over, the breeze might die in the cool of the evening, or it could be the forerunner of a long blow and we'd be stuck there. According to the chart there was no useful shelter between us and Namu, some 30 miles away. I figured that if we hurried, we would be able to get there before midnight. What should we do? We made the wrong choice. We should have taken the anchor to shore and run a stern line to the cables that hung down by the entrance. Instead, we left and sailed until dark with the wind right on our nose. We doused the sails as the night wore on and the current turned against us. There was no doubt about it; Burke Channel knew who was the boss. Sometimes it seemed that the outline of a mountaintop stayed in the same spot forever. It took us seven hours to travel the last 10 miles of that passageway.

I hung over the bow and pointed out logs that loomed, glowing green or red from the running lights, before sliding quietly on by. Paul clung to the tiller and struggled to understand my signals. Now and then we came upon a tangle of floating kelp. Sometimes he shut down the engine, but then it would refuse to start. We took to relying on my sense of direction and the outline of the nearby hills because the chart indicated a shoreline clear of reefs. Travel became an act of faith.

We reached the glaring lights of Namu at 5:30 in the morning. Too tired to eat anything but a small bowl of granola, we fell into bed and slept soundly right through the hubbub of boats coming and going, not waking until two in the afternoon. Evening dinner at the commissary never tasted better. After eating we took a stroll up the pathway that leads to the lake. The broken shards of clamshells and black earth underfoot suggested that the mound we had to climb to get near the stream was an old kitchen midden. Of course, the Natives would have come here to harvest salmon.

A sense of déjà vu overcame me. The White person's need to own and occupy one specific bit of land had again collided with the food-gathering habits of Native people. These tribes owned, by tradition, a number of places, moving between them regularly as the seasons turned, from halibut grounds to eulachon runs to salmon streams and all the various crops in between. When foreigners arrived and found a place unoccupied, they felt justified in assuming nobody wanted it.

It was not until 1993 that I read, in Kenneth Campbell's excellent book *North Coast Odyssey,* that archaeologists had discovered evidence that the site where Namu is located has been occupied for nearly 10,000 years. Robert Draney came here in 1893 to build a salmon cannery and found Heiltsuk smokehouses. The Native use of this place went back so far that in the lower level of the dig, the archaeologists found microblades. These obsidian chips set along a hardened wooden shaft had been used by North Coast people in early prehistoric times. Now, descendants of these early tribes no longer found work in the defunct cannery. There was little left to put into cans.

But for the time being, travellers like us, and weary fishermen, were grateful for the chance to tie up to the floats. When we woke next morning I tackled the shopping and laundry needs while Paul settled into the task of solving the engine problem. He found that the regulator was malfunctioning and there was no electrician on-site. It was clear the engine required major work before we could fulfill our dreams of exploring more of this glorious BC coastline. Paul vowed that he'd spend however long it took to get the engine functioning efficiently. As for myself, I was committed to taking a sabbatical in the coming school year, so change was all around us.

Of course, we fished our way south and had our usual good luck, but when it came time to pass Cape Caution, we were stymied. We were hemmed in by fog, lots of it. With no sophisticated navigation devices, we were stuck with our compass, our echo sounder, my eyes and Paul's ears. We huddled in Jones Cove for a few days in faint hope that the fog would clear, but each morning we

Wood Duck tied to the meandering floats at Namu, after running all night to get there.

woke to see it still hanging around, dripping from the rigging and outlining every spiderweb in tiny pearls. Somehow these little spiders come all the way across the water to make their flytraps on the lifelines. They weave their magic in the late summer if you spend more than a day at an anchorage. But the beauty of their handiwork did little to offset the gloom of our surroundings.

After dark I usually read out loud beside the tiny kerosene lamp. This had become an evening ritual; Paul did the dishes, maintained fishing gear or did whatever small job he had on hand while I read to him. I loved revisiting books about this treasured coast and spent some time each winter gathering titles that I thought he would enjoy. Like most gifted dyslexics, his strong point was not reading, but he loved this sharing time. We had been enjoying *The Curve of Time* when Paul made the comment that we were in some ways not unlike Muriel Wylie Blanchet, the author, in that we travelled with primitive navigational equipment and relied on a spotter hanging over the bow when we ventured into new places. Now, in Jones Cove, Paul stopped stirring the cups of hot chocolate he had been making, cocked his head on one side and said, "You know, June, if this fog keeps up, we'll soon run out of books. There has to be some way that we can continue our journey."

"Let me take another look at our route," I replied. He moved the cocoa mugs and handed me the chart. I spread it out on the galley table, looked at it for a while and then reached for the flashlight. "Hey, I think I've got it."

And there it was, right before our eyes. The underwater coastline from Egg Island, out around Cape Caution and as far down as McEwan Rock has a fairly even contour. Nearby Miles Inlet would be our destination. Once we located Egg Island, with its helpful lighthouse and foghorn, we could use our echo sounder and weave back and forth over the 48-fathom line to get past Cape Caution.

This 48-fathom "line" is not actually a line at all, but as the depth increases from shore to deep ocean bottom, the cartographer indicates common depths by using lines made up of various combinations of dots and dashes. Close to the shore, the six-fathom line consists of three dashes and a space, and the area between this line and the shore is coloured pale blue. Since each fathom measures six feet, mariners know they are in 36 feet of water or less. The next delicate line is made up of a dot and a dash alternating along its length. This hems in the approximate 12-fathom depth. Beyond this is a line made up of two dots and a dash; the soundings on either side range around 24 fathoms. The line I planned to use is five dots interspaced by a solid section. Depths on either side go from 46 to 52 fathoms. With careful monitoring we would be able to zigzag across this general area and get to our destination.

I showed Paul what I had found. He grinned and said, "You're the navigator, June. If you think we can make this work, let's go for it. But it would be a safer bet if we didn't have to contend with too much wind."

Morning came damply with no breeze to clear away the fog. So we set out with ghosts of the early explorers swirling in our misty wake. Without charts they had been forced to rely on sight, hearing and the lead line that a crew member heaved forward and let run through his fingers, counting the fathom knots until it hit bottom. A small cup filled with tallow was attached to the elongated lead weight at the end of the line. Where the tallow hit the ocean floor, it picked up loose bits, giving the navigator an idea of the texture of the bottom. When seashells appeared, he knew he was nearing the shallows.

We were spared all this heaving of a cold, dripping line, but we got similar results from our echo sounder, which fired off pulses of sound that bounced back to a receiver located on the bottom of the hull. Bats know all about this method of avoiding collisions in midair. The quicker the echo, the closer the obstruction; the sharper the echo, the harder the surface. So it was with our sounder. Its face was circular, much like the face of a clock. A small light blinked opposite the indicated depth. If the surface of the ocean floor was solid rock, there was a bright clear flash. If the bottom was muddy, the flash was speckled and less precise. We also had a proper weight for sounding by hand that Paul had cast in bronze, but we were both thankful that the electrical one worked.

We were also grateful that the wind didn't rise along with the sun. The usual Pacific swells had the boat rolling gently, so we kept a hand on our coffee cups, partly to avoid spills and partly to keep our fingers warm. Fog has a way of creeping through gaps in clothing, so we piled on extra sweaters and donned our rain gear. Even the gulls huddled on drift logs with snugly folded wings and necks scrunched down into their collars, hardly bothering to turn their heads as we putted on by. The only creatures that looked happy were the dip-chicks and diving birds that didn't need to see the far horizon. What mattered fog to them?

But it mattered to us on that day, because passing Cape Caution was still the challenge. As befits the area, we moved forward cautiously. Judging by the compass headings, it was soon apparent that we were being swept steadily onshore by the Pacific swells—a quarter mile for every two miles of forward progress—but the echo sounder and regular corrections kept us safe. In retrospect, I should have compensated for this, but I was not sure how long the phenomenon would persist. So we made do with what I call "gumboot" navigation. Not fancy, but workable. The fact that we could only travel at just over four knots made it a tedious, drawn-out trip. We kept going back and forth, monitoring the depths, with our eyes and ears hard at work.

Just before I expected it, we almost ploughed right into McEwan Rock. I had thought we were a little more to seaward of it, but Paul heard the swells gurgling and hissing onshore before he could see them. The little island loomed out of the fog, almost bare of growth but neatly marked with a flashing white light. We noted the triple blink of the light and timed the interval between flashes. It was, as the chart indicated, Gp Fl (3) 12 sec 62 ft. Such reassurance was comforting to us. We knew right where we were.

I used our deviation table to calculate the next heading. We needed to make an abrupt left turn that would take us directly into Miles Inlet. The entryway was funnel-shaped, with rocks abounding on both sides. I could not bring myself to add 23 degrees to the heading indicated on the chart, so I called for a correction of about 19 degrees and we moved slowly toward the shore.

The tip of a weed-capped rock appeared out of the mist with water surging over it. Paul swung the helm just before the boat collided with Morphy Rock. Not good news, so we retreated to McEwan and I added the full 23 degrees to our heading. This time we found the entrance channel and slid gratefully into it. The deviation table we had slaved over on our way upcoast had worked! Never again would I doubt it. At least, not until Paul moved the compass farther aft.

Next morning brought sunshine. If we had waited another day before making the trip down from Jones Cove, it would have been an easy sail. But we had challenged the fog demons, brushed them firmly aside and made our way safely past Cape Caution. Now we were ready to explore parts of the lower coastline, revisit old favourites and venture into new ones.

7 BLUNDEN HARBOUR

It was Emily Carr's artwork that lured us to Blunden Harbour. I had long admired her colourful paintings of First Nations villages. At a time when others scoffed at things Native, she recognized the skilled artistry of their cedar canoes, totems and houses and undertook many hazardous journeys to record this beauty before it rotted away. Among the many pictures done by this brave woman was one of Blunden Harbour. It showed the view along the boardwalk in front of the longhouses, with carved welcome figures stretching their upturned hands toward visitors coming ashore. The very name of the place filled me with wonder.

The year Paul and I visited, there remained just one small cabin above the white shell beach, the ends of peeled logs stuck out from among the berry bushes, and on the beach in front lay a lonely gillnet boat. I took a photo of the old boat for the memories it evoked of fishing boats that I had known and loved when I was a child. What we did not know was that in behind the raggedy little cabin, the remains of longhouses were hidden away under a thicket of salmonberries. The logs we saw above the beach were the ends of the huge timbers that had supported the roofs; among them were the remnants of the boardwalk that Emily had featured in her painting.

I returned to Blunden Harbour in my own sailboat eight years later with a friend, Andy Andrews, and his dog, a bitch that was mostly wolf. We could see that someone had slashed a pathway

When we reached Blunden Harbour, the site of the welcoming men figures famously painted by Emily Carr, all that seemed to remain of the original village were a few longhouse support posts hanging out above the white shell beach. This shack from a later era has since burned to the ground.

into the remains of a collapsed longhouse, so we scrambled eagerly up the steep bank. The whole structure had fallen toward the water. To get inside we had to duck under the edge of the roof, which supported a growth of moss and young trees. The split cedar shakes that had kept this house dry for many years were an astonishing size: 33 inches wide, 3 inches thick and 8 feet long! These days you would be hard pressed to find virgin timber that could provide such amazing shingles.

We crept down into the dusty charcoal hollow in the centre of the house, where cooking fires had burned many years ago, and saw, near the back wall, the incongruous remains of an old iron bedstead. Above our heads ran beautifully fluted longitudinal roof beams. Between them the shakes drooped under the weight of the growth on top. Cracks here and there admitted shafts of light speckled with dust motes. As we squatted amidst this fallen glory, the dog's hackles rose and she emitted a blood-curdling howl that went on and on. I have to admit that the hairs on the back of my neck rose in response. Andy hurried out of the cave with her, but I could not leave. A presence surrounded me.

Nothing remained of the carved wooden figures and bowls that so entranced Muriel Blanchet when she was there with her children in the mid-1920s. The two-headed serpent, Sisiutl, which lay along the back platform, was gone, as were the huge carved wooden serving containers held in the outstretched paws of pairs of birds or animals. The rear support posts with carved leering faces had either fallen into the floor or been taken away by scavengers to be sold to museums worldwide. No wonder the dog scuttled out of the place. It had been violated, and the spirits were still angry. They muttered and murmured in the cold, dusty corners. Yet, amid the swirling sounds, there was an undercurrent of soft drumming and chanting as though the memories of longhouse gatherings still permeated the structure. Their persistence gave hope for the future.

Inside the collapsed longhouse at Blunden Harbour, you can just make out the adze marks running around and along the support log.

I came out into the daylight filled with wonder. Andy and his dog were exploring the beachfront where, amid the glare of broken clamshells, he was finding the blue glass trading beads for which Native people had decimated the sea otter population to fill the coffers of entrepreneurs who carried their loot by sail to market in Cathay.

I was sorry that salmonberry bushes hid the longhouse when Paul and I were here. He would have been floored by the workmanship on the beams and by the dimensions of the cedar shakes that covered the roof. But other gifts of wonder awaited us on that trip.

Two small islets divide the inner bay at Blunden Harbour. The one farthest from the settlement is Grave Island. After we had finished our usual firewood-gathering trip to the beach, I said, "Let's go and see if that one is anything like the burial island at Mamalilaculla." But the trees were nondescript, and there was no sign from the water that the island was anything but a shelter for otters.

"Let's try the one nearest the village site," said Paul. "The trees look a lot healthier, and I can see something up in the branches."

"Oh, wow! Do you think we've finally found bentwood boxes still in trees?"

The first time we roamed an ancient burial island, we had found two such boxes that had fallen among the salal bushes on the ground. The cedar ropes that tied them to the branches above had succumbed to wind and weather. We were so in awe that we did not presume to touch the boxes, but by moving aside the salal leaves we could see bones and parts of deteriorating skulls inside the shattered remnants of the delicate cedar planks that had been steamed, bent and crafted years ago to make a personal container. These "trunks," as it were, had contained the possessions of the owners while they were alive and served as coffins when they died.

When Paul finally drew the rowboat near the rocky shore of the small islet, we spotted not boxes, but several dresser drawers lashed to pairs of branches. These containers were only large enough to contain the bodies of small children. What terrible disaster had befallen them? Diphtheria, which had been so fatal to both White and Native children at Cortes Island during the early years of the 20th century, or any similar plague could have killed these youngsters.

On the other side of this small islet were more such containers, and in amongst the rocks below the trees I spotted an abalone button jammed in a crevice. Traditionally, chiefs had been fitted into their own bentwood boxes that were then wrapped in their ceremonial button blankets and put up in a tree alone rather than in a tree containing family members. How many years had it been since this honoured personage was hoisted up into the waiting arms above? Nothing remained of his box or bones except the one shining button. Yet in nearby trees were dresser drawers carefully mounted in the ancient manner.

Our poignant discovery left us both shaken. We knew that school-aged children had been taken away to residential schools to be made into "White people," leaving behind the elders, parents and babies. If death had stalked the longhouses, robbing a culture of its future, it was easy to see why whole families had moved to places like Alert Bay, where they could at least be nearer to the schools where the older children lived—and perhaps nearer to the hospital, where there was some hope of recovery from the diseases that wrought such havoc.

We were curious to see if the Whites' insistence on mausoleums and coffins had influenced this village. It seemed doubtful, given the boxes in the trees, but we pushed our way through the dense growth of salal bushes and found two small log buildings, hidden in the shadows, with intact roofs and doors. What joy to find that the bones of these ancestors had been left undisturbed by grave robbers! Back at the boat, we mulled over our discovery. It would be unthinkable to share the news about the site with anyone else, given that artifact seekers regularly plunder these places.

I am sad to say that in 2006, 26 years after our visit, I learned that someone had raided these two sacred places. One coffin was dragged outside and the lid was ripped off, exposing the skeleton of a male dressed in an inexpensive polyester suit that was probably bought for the occasion. Obviously someone loved him and cared enough that he look presentable when he was laid to rest. Should any of his descendants return to this burial place and find such an unspeakable violation, their rage would be understandable. We are not talking about excavating the Valley of the Kings in Egypt; these graves are not more than 40 years old. Imagine the outcry in a White community if graves and cemeteries were treated in a similar manner. It is no wonder that Native anger at being treated as second-class citizens is gaining strength.

At the time we were there, however, things were as they should have been, so we went on our way. At that point our trip began to take on some urgency. In just a handful of days I was scheduled to fly to the UK with my 82-year-old father. I planned to take a year off teaching so I could finish my master's degree at Western Washington University in Bellingham. Lectures did not begin until the third week in September, so my father had offered to take me to England for a three-week visit. Among other places, he wanted to see the old Roman fort town of Caerleon, in south Wales, where he had been born and where he and his chums had played gladiator in the remnants of the coliseum. How could I say no to an offer like that? Needless to say, Paul was not overjoyed that I was about to jump ship, but my dad's offer was too good to turn down. He was also going to support me during my leave from teaching, so I was rather in his debt.

Paul and I hurried down Johnstone Strait, intending to pause at Campbell River, where I would catch the bus back to Vancouver, leaving Paul to return to his mooring in the Fraser River by himself, as he had done countless times in the past.

It was late in the day when we approached Turn Island at a bend in the strait near Chatham Point lighthouse. The weather forecast was for strong southeast winds to arrive during the night, so we needed to find a secure anchorage out of the wind. We had been behind Turn Island before, but the logging camp that flourished there used many different parts of the bay for booming their logs. We knew it was a gamble, but we hoped to find a spot to fit our needs.

Just as we were about to head in behind the island, Paul noticed a seagull swerve in its flight and drop down over some disturbance on the surface of the water near the shore. "Let's take a minute to see what that activity is all about," he said. "I'll bet there's a feeding salmon over there."

As he changed course, I handed him his rod and scrambled up near the bow so that I could warn him of underwater obstructions. He was beginning to make a pass along the shore when I yelped, "Head out, head out, There's a rock just below the surface."

He put the helm hard over and gave the engine a burst of speed to lift the fishing line up over the obstruction. Suddenly, his rod bent sharply and the reel began to sing. He jammed the motor into neutral and held the rod straight up. The tip bobbed. We hadn't caught bottom—it was a strike! The seagull had alerted us to a salmon feeding on a small school of herring, and the rapid change in direction of Paul's lure had looked to the fish like escaping dinner.

After the usual struggle, we ended up with a 43-pound spring salmon bleeding out in the cockpit. Then we headed in behind Turn Island. It looked like most of the good anchoring spots were filled with log booms, and Paul still had to row ashore to harvest alder for the smoker, so we checked out the little bay on the inner side of the island. As usual, Paul stopped the motor while we made our decision. The echo sounder gave off sharp blips of light, which made it look like the bottom was rock infested. I suggested we go across the way, where sea grasses indicated a bit of mud, but when Paul tried to start the engine it refused to fire. By this time the current that swept into the passageway was making its presence known, and we were drifting back in the direction from which we had come. Paul dropped the anchor right there. It held, so he scrambled into the dinghy and rowed ashore.

I set to work cleaning and cutting up the huge salmon before it got too dark to see what I was doing. At one point I glanced over to the shore and saw that we were adrift, so I quickly rinsed my slippery hands over the side, hurried forward to lift the anchor, checked the flukes for debris and let it down again. This time it held.

We were not in an ideal position by any means. The current raced past us, and the building power of the wind kept the hull veering from one side to the other, but with no engine we were stuck there. This was turning out to be the night from hell.

Paul got back to the boat after dark with his precious load of green alder. We checked the depth and found we were in over 10 fathoms of water, so he let out all 230 feet of anchor line, and we prayed that our hook would hold. I had already salted the salmon, so Paul fixed us hot rum while I prepared a light supper. We set the alarm for three so I could rinse off the salt and lay the fish out to air-dry before smoking. It was fortunate the seagulls didn't fly after dark, because the back deck held a veritable feast.

What did fly all night was the boat. It sailed back and forth with each blast of wind. The night was utterly black. Neither of us slept deeply in those conditions, and we took turns going up on the bow to check the firmness of the line to the anchor that kept us from being swept away. Bright ribbons of phosphorescence streamed back in the current, so we could follow the curve of the line for more than 30 feet before the eerie green light faded.

By eight o'clock in the morning we had the stove going with the first load of fish ready in the smoker. The fire had developed a fine bed of coals, so Paul began to feed it with small chunks of green alder, and I plugged the top of the smokestack to direct the scented smoke into the box that rested neatly on top of the cabin roof. Then he set to work figuring out what was the matter with the engine. By late morning he had determined that no current was passing through the field windings in the starting motor. This meant that the repair job could not be done on board—not even by a mechanical genius like him. This set us back on our heels.

After the night we had put in, followed by his troubleshooting, Paul was exhausted. He climbed into the bunk for a nap. I stayed up to feed alder to the stove, all the while puzzling over how I was going to catch that bus to Vancouver. I stared at the engine. It was a small unit, barely larger than the engine of a full-sized garden Rototiller. Then it occurred to me that you could start a Rototiller with a rope wound around the little notched wheel on the front of the shaft. Why couldn't we do that with this motor?

I was so excited that I shook Paul awake. At that moment I was not a popular crew member. My inspiration could have waited a little longer, but the deed was done.

Paul removed the flywheel cover, wrapped a 3/8th-inch line around the alternator pulley and gave a little tug on the line. The resistance he felt told him that this might work to spin the engine. The problem was going to be the confined space. Right above him was the ship's radio telephone. Any pull he made would have to be short and brisk. He set the choke, turned on the key and gave the rope a quick pull. The engine started as if nothing had ever been wrong. Hallelujah! We pulled up our anchor and were on our way.

The current was running against us. Seymour Narrows was only 20 miles away, but it would be six in the evening before slack water. We were afraid to turn the engine off, so we pulled out of our safe haven, trailing a cloud of aromatic smoke, and began a leisurely trickle along the shoreline down the strait. We were out of the opposing current, so we lingered here and there to drag a fishing line.

As the tide turned, our boat broke through the swirls and eddies in the narrows and we found the southeast wind waiting for us, but it was greatly diminished from the previous night. We slogged along through building slop as the current began to meet the oncoming wind. Discovery Passage can be a nasty bit of work in these conditions, but our engine never faltered. It was nearly 10 p.m. before we tied snugly to the fishermen's float in the harbour. But it was a cozy night, with the stove keeping us warm while the smoker did its job on the top deck, filling the marina with tantalizing smells.

Next morning Paul set off with the starting motor tucked under his arm to find someone to fix it while I began packing canning jars with some of the fish I had smoked the night before. When Paul returned, I took the time to review with him the canning method, since he was to be left with that chore. I packaged up a bundle of the fragrant salmon, tucked it into my packsack and blithely set off on the bus for my big adventure, not realizing that I was sowing seeds of discontent in our relationship. Foresight is never as efficient as hindsight, and most of us lack the services of a crystal ball.

8 GETTING INTO GEAR

Throughout the next two winters, Paul and I often found ourselves busy with our separate interests. He was occupied with the Kermath engine that had come with *Wood Duck*. He loved the little engine, which he now knew intimately and which certainly fit his boat, but it was in dire need of work if we were to fulfill our dream of exploring the Queen Charlotte Islands. He discovered that production of the small Kermath had ceased about 40 years earlier, although larger versions were still being built in Michigan for industrial use. He also learned that Hercules parts would fit the Kermath, which would help in a pinch, and he did get the cylinders rebored and installed new rings so the engine would lose its voracious appetite for oil. He also built and plumbed in a freshwater tank so we no longer had to rely on a collapsible plastic bag for drinking water.

Meanwhile, I spent the school year commuting from Abbotsford to the university at Bellingham in Washington State, a pleasant drive through farming country. I loved being a student again, but my encroaching deafness was a constant source of stress. I studied, did my reading and writing, filled the weekends with boat racing and spent time with Paul, but my mind was often distracted by the demands I faced. My dad typed all of my essays and did the shopping and quite a bit of the cooking.

My thesis kept me busy until after midsummer, so Paul went off to Cortes on his own. He put *Wood Duck* on the tidal grid so he could work on the hull, and he also helped Warren and Ginny Tormey with their garden. When I finally completed my degree, I felt that I owed my father a special holiday, so I loaded him into my little sailboat and we ventured up the coast as far as Cortes Island, where he had lived 25 of his retirement years with my mother, and visited many of the places that he remembered. He spent a week living alone on the boat at the Cortes Bay Marina, where the Seattle Yacht Club now has its outstation, while I took a short trip with Paul as far as Cameleon Harbour.

When it came time to make the journey back to the city, our two boats travelled as a team. We rafted together at night in Pender Harbour near Harry Dusenbury's float, which had figured so largely in my dad's travels up the coast when I was a child. After we left Gibsons, Paul headed for the North Arm of the Fraser River, while Dad and I went around the north side of Bowen Island on our way to False Creek. As usual, Paul was trailing a fishing line, so when I saw him stop alongside Keats Island, I assumed he'd lucked into a salmon. His boat stayed in one spot for a while, but I was not worried. Although I had his walkie-talkie on board, I never used it because I couldn't hear what was being said. I should have activated it and handed it to my dad, but the thought never crossed my mind.

As it turned out, Paul's engine had quit, the wind was getting up, and he was concerned. If I had been with him, we would have either sailed to the mouth of the Fraser and begged a tow or sailed back to Gibsons and caught the bus home, but I was a sailboat racer who had learned to move with just the power of the sails. Paul depended on having an engine, so he felt truly alone out there. After a struggle, he did manage to get the engine going again and powered up the river to his mooring.

When I phoned him the next evening, he accused me of abandoning him, but I told Paul that I didn't see how we could have helped him with his engine. With my 83-year-old father in my small boat, I had been worried that the building wind would cause trouble when we got to the turbulent waters near Point Atkinson, and I knew that Paul would solve his problem as he had before. I could see no way I would have done things differently.

It was not an auspicious start to our winter of preparation for the trip to the Charlottes. Had we not both been totally committed to this adventure, I think we would have parted company that fall. As it was, I kept coming in to visit him on the weekends when I had races with my all-female crew. And the day after school ended in June, we set off on our adventure.

Unlike our previous trips, this one moved swiftly. By July 4 we were at Port McNeill, having burned an astonishing 27 litres of fuel. This was a record for us, as we usually meandered along, often with the headsail adding its little bit of pull. When we tied to the float at Port McNeill, we were pleased to see *Lawana*, a charming old boat from Seattle that was home to the "pair of Jeans," Jean and Eugene, whom we had met the previous summer. When we told them of our plans, they happily dragged out their charts and shared with us some of their favourite anchorages on the route upcoast.

We used the first of these the next evening. Our route took us up Browning Passage between Nigei and Balaklava islands. Just after Queen Charlotte Strait came into full view, we spotted the metal sign on our left that marked the entrance. This was one of those safe harbours known only to the commercial salmon fishing fleet. The marker was an arrow painted on a chunk of corrugated metal nailed to wooden braces on the trunk of a tree. A searchlight could pick out its welcome on the darkest, stormiest night. There was a mate on the opposite side of the narrow passageway, but the metal plate had long since fallen from the two-by-four frame.

The entryway was beautiful. We wriggled past slate-coloured sandstone islets capped with tangled scrubby trees. The sheltered inner bay was long and narrow, opening up into a larger bay spiked with ugly logs, an unwholesome-looking spot. We dropped the anchor just past the entryway before hopping into the dinghy to search for firewood along the shore. The tide was really high, so we looked for dead branches hanging from the surrounding trees. Paul spotted a likely looking one that turned out to be a weathered yew. The wood is tough as steel, so I held the boat as still as I could while he struggled to cut off several branches. We loved this fuel because it gave off a lovely aromatic smoke and burned for hours.

Once the woodcutting was done, we rowed around, exploring our sanctuary. We were pleased to find a small, clamshell-covered beach among the small islands that spoke of long-ago feasts by Native people. They, too, had sought shelter here on their journeys along this rugged shoreline.

Near the entryway to the cove we spotted a foot-long grey worm wriggling just below the surface. He moved quickly through the water with his many tiny feet paddling furiously. Just past him I saw strange little transparent, wafer-thin, bluish-purple jellyfish, each with a small sail arching up in the centre. The evening breeze seemed to have wafted them into our shelter. Some of them had flipped upside down. They were edged with tiny cilia and had streamers that hung down below, and my first thought was that they were miniature Portuguese men-of-war. In no time our rowboat was surrounded by these fairy creatures.

It was not until I read Terry Glavin's book *The Last Great Sea* that I learned these mysterious floaters are by-the-wind-sailors, or *Velella*, which is a thoroughly charming name that rolls around on your tongue. They are not one being at all, but a symbiotic array of three distinct colonies of animals. According to Glavin, "One colony forms the sail, rising amidships on a hard ridged mast that holds the sloop into the wind. Another colony forms the translucent blue hull, which serves as a digestive system. The third colony, composed of hanging stingers, forms the tiny sloop's keel." They are found anywhere between Hawaii and the string of islands that stretches from Alaska to Russia. They always form flotillas and sail off together on their odyssey. The wonder is that these tiny creatures find each other and set up such a divinely co-operative "village." The only reason we met them in that lonely bay was that El Niño had swept closer to the BC coast that year, bringing with it many more treasures for us to discover.

The next morning, as we headed out early on our way to Cape Caution, we came upon great flocks of these tiny creatures. Our wake cut through them, flipping some upside down, and I wondered if they would ever right themselves. Given that their group intelligence had gotten them this far on their journey, it seemed likely they had developed a way to undo our mischief.

The wind rose with the warmth of the sun, and when Egg Island came abeam we were reaching along under sail at four knots. Suppertime found us snugly anchored behind Fury Island. The rocky islets that form this shelter keep out the Pacific swells until the tide rises enough to cover the beaches, which glow with white barnacle shells even after dark. That night we were lulled asleep by the murmur of waves that rolled in between the islands and gently rocked our hull.

We felt so pleased with our progress that we made a lazy start the next morning and did a little fishing, with the engine just ticking over quietly and the fishing rods spread out like wings from the rod holders on the back railing of the boat. This kept our speed at about three knots. The fishing lure was held down under the water by a device called a Deep Six. When a fish hit the bait, it tripped the Deep Six so that the line rose to the surface. This caused a flurry of activity, because we had to manhandle the other line on board right away in case the fish dove to one side and tangled the gear together. Occasionally we reeled the line in to find nothing but a great bundle of seaweed on the end, and one day we snagged a fishing company's flag. But the day we left Fury Island, our efforts paid off. By the time we wormed our way into Kwakume Inlet, a few miles downcoast from Namu, we had four nice fish to eat or to can for our winter food supply.

Sailing and slowing down to fish certainly helped stretch our fuel supply; when we got to the fuelling float at Namu, our tank took only 6.7 gallons of gas—that was all we had consumed since leaving Port McNeill. We tied overnight at Namu, where the floats were jam-packed with gillnet boats waiting for the official opening of the season in three days. It was like a small floating village, humming with anticipation. Boats sparkled with new paint. Children scampered around. A few women stood talking here and there. Dogs barked. Men were either hard at work repairing gear or standing in groups with beer bottles in their hands. Social

Happy sailing on a sparkling day, taking full advantage of the wind.

activity on the docks continued well into the night. Next morning, youngsters rowed around the harbour chattering to each other as they gathered floating beer bottles to take back to the store for the bottle deposits.

Morning dawned crisp and clear with a helpful southeast breeze to push us along. Paul had made a new whisker pole for this trip, so we set the mainsail to starboard, attached one end of the new pole to the fitting on the leading edge of the mast, clipped the other end to the free corner of the headsail and pushed the end of the pole out to port. Now our boat had wings on both sides. We took full advantage of the wind as we soared along Fisher Channel. An abrupt left turn into Lama Passage brought us to an area we had never seen before.

There is a special delight that comes with venturing into unknown territory. There is also a lot of satisfaction in doing it right. Our charts revealed quantities of information. We could identify each headland based on the lines of elevation defining it. For a sharp incline, the lines on the chart were close together, whereas for a gentle incline the lines were well spaced. The other handy thing was that aids to navigation, such as lighthouses and beacons, were clearly marked. Once we spotted these, we knew exactly where we were. The hardest part was trying to find an opening between islands. Sometimes we had to be patient until paler tones in the distance became clear. At first we saw only a continuous shoreline, but gradually, as we drew near, we would recognize the fading of detail that separated one from the other.

Our trip up Lama Passage took us around a gentle curve in the shoreline, through a narrows and out past Story Point. Ahead of us, on our left, we could see the docks and buildings of Bella Bella, a sizeable settlement of 60-odd houses with some newer split-level housing stretching off downcoast. After our day of sailing there was no need to search for a gas float, so we moved slowly along the shoreline until we saw the markers for the small boat harbour. The entry was daunting as it twisted between reefs and a pair of small islands—like going into Silva Bay just south of Nanaimo. I stood out near the bow to watch for shallows as we sneaked in past the green marker, made a left turn and watched for an opening amongst the many boats along the fingers that stretched toward us.

We had no sooner tied off the lines and gone below to clean up than we heard a chatter of young voices and a clunk on our stern. Sure enough, a bevy of small children were clambering into our dinghy and getting out the oars.

I shouted, "Hey, what do you think you're doing?"

They looked thoroughly startled that anyone would question their actions. I explained that we were going to need that rowboat, handed out some cookies and sent them on their way. Paul moved temptation around to the offside of our bow and snugged it there beside a fender to protect the hull.

I had heard about the Native custom of giving young children free rein in the world, but this was my first encounter with such relaxed discipline. According to Lester Peterson in his wonderful book *The Story of the Sechelt Nation,* the Sechelt elders felt that it was wrong to make a young child fearful of anything. Children were encouraged to behave, but not disciplined physically, because learning to fear as the result of being punished would inhibit them in their interaction with the world. Fearlessness was valued above all else.

After our precious rowboat was secure, we set off to investigate the village. Partway along the float I stopped in my tracks. "Paul, there's the *Porpoise 3*. I've chased after that sailboat in so many races. I wonder which way they are going?" I rapped on the hull, but when I got no response I said, "I'd really like to talk to Bill Killam. I don't know if they have just arrived or whether they are leaving, and I'd hate to miss a chance to pick his brains before he goes. Also I'm nervous about leaving the dinghy. Could you go on without me and I'll hang around here?"

He went off alone for a look around and to find a store, while I went back to write a note to leave on the *Porpoise*.

It started raining, but I managed to find a dry spot for my note and went back to cover our boat and feed the fire. My mentor, Gerry, of Storch Sails, had made us a great boat tent for this trip. It went right from the forward end of the cabin to the stern, with a hole to accommodate our chimney. There was a zipper on either side of the cockpit so that we could step onboard without getting a collar full of rainwater. With the cover in place, it was much easier to keep the cabin dry and fresh with the wood heater going and the hatch ajar. I made a nest for myself on the settee and enjoyed the chance to read for a while.

When I heard the whiz of a zipper and felt the boat tilt, I swung my feet to the floor, and there was Paul, dripping on the back deck. "Oh man," he said. "That is some downpour. I wish I'd taken my rain gear." He struggled out of his wet jacket and hung it under the awning to drain.

"I'll fix you a cup of hot tea," I said, "and you can tell me all about the big metropolis of Bella Bella."

He flopped down on the opposite seat and took a comb to his hair. "Well, this end of it is a mess. It must be the old part of town. There were more burned-out houses than usable ones and discarded stuff everywhere. I found the store—it's a co-op—and I was able to get the lamp oil. There was little fresh produce because the freighter doesn't come for a few days. But I did find a small cabbage. It's a good thing we have some sprouts on the go. But most of the village sure is a depressing sort of a place. Maybe it's just the rain, but I wouldn't want to spend my life here."

Just then there came a rap on the hull. I peeked out under the awning to find Bill Killam squatting on the float. "Hi, June," he said. "Good to see you. We were asleep when you came by earlier. My wife and I just got in from the Charlottes, and after that 16-hour run, we needed a nap. Come over for a visit after supper and we'll have a glass of wine and tell you all about it."

"Oh, wow," I replied. "That's just what we needed to hear. We're headed there ourselves. We'd be delighted with any advice you can give us. See you later." I slid back into the cabin as he rose to leave. "This is the best news ever. We are so lucky."

Porpoise 3 was the epitome of comfort and convenience compared to our little *Wood Duck*. With an inside steering position and Loran for navigation, this well-appointed racing sailboat could have made it to places like Hawaii with no trouble. It was easy to see why they had chosen the direct route from the bottom end of the Charlottes across to Milbank Sound just northwest of where we were now. Even so, it was a long haul for two people no longer in their 20s.

Bill and Kay made us feel most welcome. After Kay showed me her freezer and shower, we sank into the cushions on their settee with a sigh. This was living! The wood heater gave off a lovely glow, and we sipped glasses of wine as our conversation swung to the vital question of gathering a fuel supply. Bill agreed with our observation that there was no longer any bark to be found along the shore, because when logs were carried to the southern mills in log carrier barges, none of the bark was rubbed off and left behind in the water. He did have some excellent advice. "What you do is either look well down the beach for old knots or go rambling through the woods looking for fallen logs. If you see a bump, give it a kick with your boot. It will almost always be a knot that will break loose. Clean off the moss and bits of old bark, and you will have yourself a chunk of solid wood that will burn like coal."

Talk ranged over the parts of the islands that they had explored. I told Bill that I was unable to get one chart that I really wanted, so he rummaged through his supply and handed me his copy. "I'm not likely to need this chart again, June, so you're welcome to it. I can't see Kay or me going back there. Oh, do you have this guidebook?"

It was Neil Carey's *Guide to the Queen Charlotte Islands*, the one thing I longed for most. In the early 1980s, the guidebook-publishing mania had not yet hit this coast, and Carey's book was all there was in that field. It was mostly background information on the sights we would see, but anything was better than nothing. We were going to be relying on incomplete charting, common sense, word of mouth (if we met any mouths), our eyesight and hunches to keep us safe, because we were determined to see the outer coast of those fabled islands, and that was the area Carey knew best.

We talked about fishing for a while, and Paul offered Bill one of our fail-safe Tom Mack spoons. This small brass lure had been around for a great many years, but my son Al had updated it by gluing a strip of sparkly foil to one surface. Salmon found it irresistible. As we rose to leave, Bill reminded us to get landing permits from the tribal office at Skidegate near Queen Charlotte City (now known as Village of Queen Charlotte) before we left that area. He said that the Haida were putting watchmen at most of the old village sites where there were still totems to be seen. That was a bit like shutting the barn door one century too late, but it was certainly better than permitting any more desecration by souvenir hunters.

The rain was pounding down by the time we headed back to *Wood Duck*, all snug beneath the cover. Paul fed more fuel to the little wood heater, and we settled down comfortably while I read aloud some of Neil Carey's stories about the islands he loved so much. As well as maintaining a home at Queen Charlotte City, the Careys had a cabin at Puffin Cove, about two-thirds of the way down the west side of Moresby Island. Betty Carey regularly explored that rugged coast in her dugout canoe, and their stories fascinated us.

9 A NEAR DISASTER

The next morning dawned bright and beautiful. After bailing gallons of rainwater out of the dinghy, we powered up, moved out of Bella Bella boat harbour and rounded the point on our way to the open Pacific. We had studied the chart the night before and decided to wriggle our way through a backdoor route rather than hazard the open waters of Milbank Sound. This northern coastline is littered with many islands that provide the recreational boater with a bewildering choice of passages. There are the main channels, with all hazards marked, which are used by big ocean liners and freighters, but for a small vessel like ours there is a feast of possibilities. The charts gave us plenty of guidance. We kept a sharp lookout and felt that our speed of four and a half knots gave us plenty of time to change our minds. Paul knew from experience that his hull could travel at six knots, but he could exhaust the fuel supply in three hours at that speed. The slower rate would eke out his meagre fuel supply so that he could go almost forever. Our only concern was the lack of a fuel gauge. We did carry a couple of full two-gallon jerry cans in case the main 10-gallon tank ran dry, and even with this precaution, we tended to go from fuelling stop to fuelling stop.

So it was when we arrived at Klemtu. There was no attendant at the gas float, but a tiny round gnome of a Native man with a moon face had put his two red cans on the float in hopes of getting some fuel for his outboard. We asked him about the agent and he grunted, "Gas man gone fishing." Having imparted that news, he tossed his empty containers back into his little skiff and left.

Paul hung around the boat in hopes someone would show up, and I climbed the steepest ramp I have ever seen. There are places on the southern coast where low tide means a drop of 12 feet, but it must have been a good 20 feet here.

As soon as I reached the top of the ramp and set out along a wide wooden promenade, I was attacked by a horde of big dogs. None of them bit, but they walked up and down my body, put their paws on my shoulders, snuffled at my mouth and almost toppled me. As I staggered under the onslaught of this tumble of clowns, I was glad of the high railings on the boardwalk that kept me from pitching to the rocks below.

Klemtu had fallen on hard times. There were a few remaining buildings of the old China Hat Cannery and about 20 derelict houses linked by the walkway. The whole town seemed to be on pilings, much like the old cannery at Goose Bay. I had to step to one side when a golf cart piled with men trundled past me. They grinned and waved as they putted along their "road," and the hubbub of dogs dashed off to follow the cart, leaving me alone. I think the dogs were hoping I had something for them to eat—they were all incredibly skinny.

The next person I met on the walkway volunteered the information that there was no gas available until the barge made a delivery. Paul must have heard the same message because he soon joined me and we went looking for the store.

It was not hard to find and appeared to be the original company store, well stocked and tidy. The White storekeeper looked like a cross between an undertaker and a gunslinger of the 1890s, with his silk-backed vest, black clothing and a labelling stamp in a holster that rode on his hip like a six-shooter. There was no glimmer of a smile, no response to humour. He was a walking cadaver. But maybe being stuck in this backwater had this effect on a person. In retrospect, he could have been deaf.

If you go to Klemtu today, you will find it much changed. Tourism is replacing the primary industries that once kept this coast hopping. Also, the Native people have embraced the concept of fish farming and appear to be making a success of this enterprise. When Paul and I were there, the wild salmon were vanishing and the local canneries had been closed for years. With no reliable income and no hope for the future, the settlement was in limbo, but judging from the grins of the golf-cart crew, these fellows had retained their sense of humour.

Morning arrived in a flurry of rain with a brisk southeast wind to hurry it along. By eleven o'clock the sky lightened, so we set our sails wing and wing and ventured into the long slit of a waterway behind Princess Royal Island. Aside from the fact that the dampness found its way into the cabin, the run was a pleasure. We had been worrying that we would face a headwind in this channel, which was framed by exceedingly steep mountains with no hint of shelter along the way, but the gods were kind.

By nine in the evening we caught sight of Butedale. It was obvious by the number of buildings that this had been a huge operation in its heyday. My nautical chart, printed originally in 1950, showed three dwellings and a bunkhouse in what I took to be the Chinese section, deep into the bay on the left. There were nine buildings of various sizes near the cannery itself, and a row of five dwellings up on the hill overlooking the harbour. The grandest of these would have been for the manager and his family. There were seven other buildings down near the steamship dock, and a cluster of fuel tanks beside the waterfall that emptied Butedale Lake.

In his excellent book *North Coast Odyssey*, Kenneth Campbell reports that Butedale had its own constable and for some years was an official port of entry for international travellers. The store serviced not only the fishing folk but also the miners who were diligently exploring the local hillsides, so there would also have been an assayer in residence year-round. Although the actual cannery had long since shut down, Northland Navigation continued to make this a port of call until 1976. Since then, the rainforest had steadily reclaimed more land each passing year.

We had been told that fuel was usually available, so we approached the dilapidated float eagerly. A youngish man wearing a plastic cowboy hat supported by large, out-turned ears beckoned us into a mooring spot and waited to take our lines. This fellow was obviously no water rat: he didn't snub the line onto anything, just stood straining away on it and offered to take the other one, too! He had a lively smile and a lot to say. He spoke highly of his boss, told us that his own wife and two small ones were here, that the boat moored in front of us had just arrived and brought along another fellow to help, and that the store would open in the morning at seven o'clock and hot coffee and muffins would be available. There was no gas at the moment, but he assured us there would be some available farther along our route. His hat and manner told us that here was a naive and optimistic cowboy who followed a dream to go west to live amongst the salmon and sea otters.

In the morning rain we slipped and grabbed our way up an exceedingly steep metal ramp that led to the company store. The stock was meagre, but everything was neat and clean, with the coffee pot sitting on a barrel that served as a coffee table, surrounded by six comfortable-looking captain's chairs. Nearby was an ample collection of magazines plus a used pocketbook exchange. While she served us excellent coffee and hot muffins, the clerk told us that the new owner planned to turn the site into a fishing resort. We thought he had a chance of success in spite of the awesome rain—the slipperiness of the float, and the fish netting that had been tacked to all the wooden walkways, attested to its constancy. However, when I read *North Coast Odyssey*, I learned that the enterprising owner was seriously injured in 1985 and had to abandon his dream.

We heard a roar and hurried to the window to watch the arrival of a strange-looking narrow metal bullet of a boat with a tall skinny cabin. The roof bristled with radar and antennas, and two huge outboard engines bulged at the stern. The clerk said it had been specially built to carry supplies to the aluminum-mining town and smelter at Kitimat. This trip took the small boat up a series of narrow passages, one of which bore the frightening name of Devastation Channel. Since the boat would either be bucking into a wind or running before it, the skinny width was ideal. Its behaviour in a beam sea would be a nightmare, but maybe at top speed that would be a short-lived horror.

One of the men came into the shop and told us that we could likely get fuel at Hartley Bay, just along our route near the mouth of Douglas Channel, which led to Kitimat. We prayed that he was right about the gas and headed out into the rain. To our delight, a family of otters was playing amongst the pilings of a long defunct dock just past our mooring spot. We also paused to look at the amazing waterfall that drained Butedale Lake. Encouraged by the rain, it plunged down into the ocean, sending up a cloud of spray that would have shimmered with rainbows on a good day.

Droplets began trickling down our necks, so we set our sails wing and wing and wallowed on our way, running before yet another wet southeaster. Clouds shrouding the hilltops made for dull viewing, but at least we were not using any fuel. To make matters worse, I had decided to bring along an old set of wet-weather gear instead of my new one. I was still racing hard back home and didn't want to wreck the good set on barnacled beaches, a decision I was to regret. It seemed that my yellow slicker and pants were perpetually turned inside out and hung near the stove to dry. The cabin was small enough as it was without this extra encumbrance. I could have purchased a fisherman's set at Namu for about $150, but I didn't do so because we had sunny weather up until then, and I didn't want to waste the dollars on a set that lacked conveniences such as adjustable storm cuffs. The fisherman's set was strictly no nonsense, but it would have kept me dry.

We slogged our way along the interminable length of Princess Royal Island until we could make the turn seaward that would lead us to Whale Channel, where we'd make a right turn toward Hartley Bay. Paul was sure that by this time our main fuel tank would be nearly empty and wondered if he should break out a spare billy can so there was enough gas for the docking manoeuvre, but I slid my hand up the metal wall and found it cold almost to the top. "Paul, I'm sure we still have almost a full tank of gas."

He shook his head and laughed. "June, we're four days away from Namu. That's a long way. I think you must be mistaken."

Hartley Bay was hidden behind Promise Island. Now *that* sounded hopeful. We furled our soggy sails, Paul fired up the motor and eased in behind a floating log breakwater, and we tied up alongside the white fuel barge that turned out to be an ancient metal unit, peppered with rust but scrupulously clean. It was boat shaped and looked as though it might be self-propelled. There were two classy newer seine boats at the nearby dock, along with a well-maintained older one. A bevy of fine-looking Native fellows were hard at work. Some crew members were running their net off the drum for inspection before sending it up though a massive power block high in the rigging and down into the hold. One of them nodded in response to my smile, so I knew we were welcome.

Once we were settled, Paul went over to ask about getting fuel. A very polite fisherman asked, "D'you have a CB? Then call Golden Eagle on channel 14. He'll come and sell you some."

Paul clicked the CB button, tuned in to the right channel and we chuckled at the conversations coming over the air. It was as though we were sitting around a large campfire.

One woman asked, "Hey, Mary, d'you still have that great recipe for blueberry muffins?"

Another voice chimed in, " Johnny, you come home to supper right away." And so it went.

When there came a lull, Paul asked for Golden Eagle.

"Yup, I'll be right down as soon as I finish my meal."

So we mixed hot rum, found some nibbles and sat out on the back deck to have a look at the village. It seemed to be nearly all on pilings, connected by boardwalks. One glance at the terrain explained this. The area where the houses sat was a combination of muskeg and rock outcroppings. On either side rose low bluffs topped with scrubby trees. The rainfall must have been almost constant given the amount of water that lay in puddles all around. It reminded me of Ucluelet on the west coast of Vancouver Island.

The largest house was painted brown. With its stone fireplace and tidy finish, it could have sat on any street in any town, but instead of a lawn there was a basketball court out front. After a while a stocky Native man, neatly dressed and good-looking, came out the front door and ambled over to our boat. The deference shown him by a younger man told us that he was likely the chief. He passed the hose to Paul and turned on the fuel pump. Our "empty" tank would only accept a few gallons! When Paul handed back the hose and reached for his wallet to pay the bill of $4.20, Golden Eagle snorted and said, "Put your money away. That's not enough to even bother with the bookkeeping." We offered our profuse thanks, fired up the engine and crept away.

We sought shelter for the night behind Promise Island in an area called Coghlan Anchorage. In the morning we went ashore to collect firewood and look for clams. It rapidly became apparent that the nearby villagers loved clams as much as we did; however, they had neglected to harvest the cockles that hid themselves under seaweed. These tasty but tough morsels were plentiful, but we decided that if the locals shunned them, it must be for a good reason. We picked wild blueberries, gathered a supply of wood and rowed back to our boat.

The terrain had changed. Instead of towering mountains there were lumpy islands covered by scrubby trees, with numerous small bays and inlets for shelter. We were soon to be grateful for these nooks. When we left Coghlan Anchorage, we felt the beginnings of the first northwester since we had left Namu. By four o'clock we had to seek shelter. The chart showed a likely spot behind a group of small islands at the southern end of nearby Pitt Island. We just had a small-scale chart, but I hung over the bow, and Paul watched the echo sounder while we sneaked cautiously past the smaller islets. The depth decreased to 15 feet, then rapidly increased to about 30. Whew! That was a relief. We ventured into the bay, dropped the hook and spent a totally miserable night buffeted by winds that screamed down a valley and right through our rigging, heeling the boat first one way and then the other before moving on out of our so-called shelter.

In the morning we spotted a salmon troller anchored in a perfect place behind the tiny island at the entryway with his stabilizer poles down. He was out of the wind that had tortured us so cruelly. We had considered that spot on the way into the harbour but were fearful the wind might change direction during the night. No chance of that, it turned out. The gale continued all through the next day before it abated enough for us to move on.

We put one reef in the mainsail and rolled in the genoa so it was about half its normal size, then headed out into the dying wind. I estimated that we were facing about a 15-knot northwesterly, but it was hard to tell for sure with the large waves still running toward us. It was the first time I had handled Paul's boat in any sort of a breeze, so it took a while to adjust the sails for maximum efficiency. The main traveller was too far to windward, so I eased it to leeward. There was a big loop in the trailing edge of the headsail because there was no forward adjustment possible for the fairlead, but I could do nothing about that. Gradually we got the sails trimmed, and the boat heeled much less and began to surge forward. I could keep things nicely under control by heading upwind during the occasional gust.

We were making good progress when the forestay broke loose from the bow of the boat, allowing the genoa to flail around out of control. My heart still pounds when I think of how close we came to a watery end. I suppose it was the years of sailboat racing that told me to turn the boat downwind when the forestay broke loose. If so, it was time well spent.

As soon as the boat was safely turned around so that the wind was on our tail, Paul was able to bundle the headsail down on the deck. Then he jury-rigged a temporary forestay and we headed back to our anchorage at the south end of Pitt Island. Once we were out of the wind, Paul, practical fisherman that he was, put a fishing line in the water. The sea gods took pity on us and sent a shining salmon to supply us with food and to cheer us up. When all was secure and the boat was tidy, we inspected the damage and were horrified to find the bolts and lag screws that held the strap onto the forefoot were so badly corroded that they had snapped under the load. Paul said that the bow of his boat had been rammed at one time by a powerboat at the Fraser River marina when the skipper misjudged the current. These fittings should have been inspected and reset when the mast was replaced. This oversight nearly cost us our lives. Unseen corrosion is the biggest enemy of a saltwater sailor.

We were almost at the lower end of Banks Island. We had planned to cross Hecate Strait to the Charlottes when we reached the far end of Banks, but now we had to change our plans and head for the nearest major town, Prince Rupert, to get replacement bolts. I had not brought charts that went much beyond the end of Banks Island, except for the small-scale Loran map that wasted no ink on rocks and such-like obstacles. Perhaps we would meet another boat that could help us out with that problem. But there was no alternative: we needed a hardware store or a ship chandler if we were to travel anywhere in safety.

At five in the morning we powered our way out into the dregs of the northwest gale. By eight o'clock we were making negligible forward progress, although the engine was happily gulping fuel. The nearby shoreline of Pitt Island was irregular, with many indentations and harbours, so when the wide entrance of Port Stephens opened up on our right we pulled in behind a sheltering point. Paul dropped the anchor on a shallow ledge where we could keep an eye on the waves in hopes that the sea would die down.

The wind eased enough by noon that we were able to put in about three more hours of travel before the gusts returned. By chance, I had a large-scale chart called "Harbours of the West Coast of Pitt Island." What a relief that was! Mink Trap Bay was abeam, and deep within it was the intriguingly named Moolock Cove. That haven provided balm to our troubled souls because a walk ashore revealed a delightful waterfall and bathing pool. The air was lovely and warm and the blackflies were still in siesta (they come out for dinner at six), so we bathed in a pool that was lined with softly coated brown rocks and lay ourselves out to dry on a smooth black rocky incline. No breezes bothered us here. The hand of man had arranged this grotto, and whoever took the time and effort to deepen the pool and arrange the rocks just so has our eternal thanks. With a name like Moolock Cove, it seemed likely this was a Native sanctuary.

Clean and relaxed, we rowed back to *Wood Duck*, where the potatoes wrapped in foil were baking inside the little wood stove, and salmon steaks were waiting to be broiled over the glowing coals. For a while our cares were forgotten and life was good.

The next day we were up at four to avoid the afternoon north-westerlies. The logbook reports: "Put in a long day." Indeed we did. We approached the dock at Kitkatla, a Native village, in hopes of finding a store and gas barge, only to be met with stares and stony silence. I called out that we had broken our mast support and were in trouble. Ready hands reached out to grab our mooring lines and tie us up securely. A slim young Native man with thick lenses in his glasses left a boat repair job he was doing, led Paul along the float to a small workshop and helped him search through a box of spare bolts and screws. There was nothing that would do the trick, so we went in search of charts and advice.

Nearby, there was a troller with one pole lowered right across the float. An older man with perfect, gleaming white teeth was mending gear with the help of sons and nephews. At first he greeted us with mild sarcasm. "You mean you got this far without a chart! Do you know where you are?" He sent a youngster for a map showing the entire coast, and after we had proved that we weren't too dumb, he warmed up and couldn't do enough to help us. Time was in short supply with the fishing opening less than two hours away, but he cheerfully plucked a business envelope out of his breast pocket, stuffed the contents back where they came from, rooted around in his pants pocket for a stubby pencil and drew a diagram that showed us the route. "Don't worry," he said, "all the hazards are marked. Just follow the traffic. It's only a 45-mile trip." It occurred to me that this man likely had all the sea knowledge he could ever use permanently imprinted in his being. This was his ancestral homeland.

We heard a roar and turned to watch a float plane come alongside the dock and begin to discharge small freight. Women and children clambered down the tiny metal ladder and were handed grocery bags and packages before heading off up the ramp amid laughter and chatting. The plane paused long enough to take on empty fuel cans and parcels before returning to Prince Rupert. Apparently this was the daily shopping trip. I tried to persuade Paul to take the morning flight and do his shopping for parts at Rupert, but he was worried that he'd forget something that he needed to do the job properly.

We noticed a young Native fellow rolling a full barrel of fuel toward the ramp, and I commented to our benefactor that the man had a steep push ahead of him. He just grinned and said, "White men use slings and hoists. We use muscles." We chuckled, thanked him for his help and got ready to leave because a brisk wind was beginning to ripple the water. We decided to look for a quiet spot to anchor at the other end of Dolphin Island, away from the bright, neatly painted village. Besides the houses there was a large, new, two-storey school, a church and an older meeting hall, as well as a clinic, roads and lights fired by a generator that ran round the clock. It would have been a noisy place to spend the night. The narrow slit of a bay we found was no great shakes for peace and quiet, because the surrounding land was not high enough to deflect much of the wind, but there were no waves and the mud bottom pleased the anchor.

When we woke, we realized we had forgotten to ask about fuel, so we motored back only to find the boats had all gone fishing. I walked up the ramp and knocked on the door of a nearby house. A very old Native woman answered the door, listened to my plea and sent me to the far end of the boardwalk. Like Klemtu and Butedale, this settlement was also waiting for the fuel barge to arrive, but the puffy-faced noncommittal man at the other end of the wooden walkway said he thought he could spare about four gallons. That would be enough to take us to Rupert, so I went to get Paul. He paid generously, thanked the old fellow and away we went. Once again, Native people had come to our rescue.

The run to Prince Rupert proved to be as simple as predicted. No wind, but plenty of boats once we reached the first of many wharves. Freighters were loading grain, a new terminal was under construction at Ridley Island, and there was a coal-loading facility. Another freighter anchored in the harbour was loading whole logs. British Columbia is notorious for allowing whole logs to be shipped overseas while local pulp mills and sawmills close for lack of a dependable supply.

With so many fishing boats out on the grounds, there was plenty of room for us at the floats farthest along the waterfront. Tied just down the way from us was a slim Fraser River gillnetter, *Glimpt*, of the type built by Japanese craftsmen in the early part of the 20th century. We walked along to admire it, and a tiny man stepped out of the cabin. He told us that his boat was 30 feet long and had been built in 1930 at Steveston near the mouth of the Fraser. We asked him about the name and he chuckled, "That's Scandinavian for 'glimpse' because this boat goes so fast you just get a glimpse of it as it scoots past." It had been his home for many years and looked the part. The back deck was cluttered with precious stuff that he had saved and could not bear to throw away. He told us his name was Joe and that he was 80, so he'd had lots of years in which to build up his impressive collection of odd bits and pieces.

When we told him our troubles, he wouldn't hear of letting Paul go uptown to buy parts. "They'll rob you blind. Come on board and we'll see what bolts I have in my collection." I went back to *Wood Duck* and left them to it.

Joe had little of use, so Paul hiked into town to find what he needed. He drilled new holes in the forefoot, installed through bolts and lag screws, and then whittled wooden plugs, which he glued in to fill any gaps. With a bit of paint, the bow looked as good as new. Paul also checked any fitting on the cables that supported the mast at the sides, so we could sail without fear of a repeat performance of our near dismasting. While he was hard at work, I walked uptown to do the laundry and restock the larder.

The size and age of the various hotels, bowling alley and entertainment facilities spoke of wartime days when a staggering number of US servicemen had been posted here during the Second World War. Now the whole town looked a little tattered around the edges and drenched from the downpour of rain that was an almost daily occurrence. When I mentioned the rain to my cousin Rod, he chuckled and said, "June, when I was just a kid and working on a small five-man halibut boat, we used to go there for supplies and a layover. When I asked an old Norwegian fisherman about the weather, he told me how you could tell if it was going to be a wet day. He told me that if you could see the nearby mountain, it was going to rain, and if you couldn't see it, it was raining!"

We ended up staying in Prince Rupert for two days. So much of our two-month summer holiday was gone already that I suggested we simply get charts for Alaskan waters and go there instead. After all, we were nearly at the border of that northerly state. Paul's shoulders slumped at the idea. I think both of us knew this was likely our last trip together, so we decided to stick to our original plan. If we had to keep our visit there brief, so be it. For better or worse, Queen Charlotte Islands, here we come.

10 CROSSING HECATE

The area around Larsen Harbour, at the northern end of Banks Island, is a mixture of sandy beaches, rocks and low hills covered in tortured trees. It is also the nearest spot on the mainland to Queen Charlotte City. A fisherman at Prince Rupert had told me how to avoid the various rocks and shoals around the entrance to Larsen. Then he chuckled and said, "When you are entering the harbour there's lots of kelp, but don't let that scare you. You'll find mooring buoys inside, so you'll be safe. Good luck on your trip." With Queen Charlotte City a good 70 miles away across Hecate Strait, we were going to need plenty of that.

To see Paul's beaming face as we worked our way past the marker and spotted the mooring buoys made the navigation effort worthwhile. We spent a quiet, mosquito-filled night and got up to the call of the alarm at 3:30 to tick quietly out of the semi-dark harbour. Daylight comes much earlier this far north, and we wanted to make use of every minute available. The shore was at the indefinite distance that pre-dawn creates. The tide was low, exposing beds of kelp that consisted of twisting silky ropes supported by small brown globes trailing wafting streamers. In spite of the Prince Rupert fisherman's reassurance, I could feel my toes curling up inside my sailing boots as those ominous streamers slipped past the hull. Motoring through kelp has never been my favourite activity. When I lifted my eyes, I could see in the distance a large passenger liner, ablaze with lights, moving south. It looked like they were having an all-night party, or maybe someone had forgotten to flick off the light switch. No matter, we were on our way.

The weather forecast for the day was spot-on. A gentle breeze from the southeast allowed us to sail most of the way. Cloud formations were like those one sees on the prairies, great towering masses over the landforms. And, as on the prairies, we could see right to the horizon in all directions. It was a long slow trip, and by late afternoon we were overjoyed to see the Misty Isles rise slowly up out of their watery bed to greet us. Our dream was coming true.

The proper way to approach the gap between Moresby and Graham islands is to home in on a radio beacon or line up two range markers about 10 miles north of the entrance, run straight in to the shoreline, then turn to follow bell buoys down a fairly narrow channel between the sandbanks offshore and the rocky beach. However, both the fisherman and Bill Killam had told us that in quiet weather it was possible to cross the bar about three miles north of Sandspit if you came straight in toward a radio beacon just to the left of a green can buoy. You had to be aware of a shoal off to the right of the can buoy.

When we finally reached the area of shallow water, we made careful use of the radio direction finder and the echo sounder and motored along slowly. We seemed to be in 4 fathoms of water forever before the depth dropped again to 12 fathoms or more. You could actually see the line of demarcation between the deep and shallow water, not by colour but by wave activity. The deep water had a current running north, while little ripples covered the sandbar. We had been told that in heavy weather, turbulent waves replaced the ripples. In such conditions, this approach could be downright dangerous. But for us it was easy. All in all, it had been a restful, uneventful day. But then, maybe adventure is the last thing one should crave during a crossing of the notoriously dangerous Hecate Strait.

Much of the strait is less than 15 fathoms deep, with a tidal rise and fall of about 26 feet to add to the confusion. When storms roar in from either the north or the south, the waves generated in the bottomless ocean are compressed by the shallows. The resulting turbulence makes this one of the most dangerous waterways on earth.

The name Hecate (which should be pronounced **hek-*uh*-tay**) is evocative. This Greek deity's role changed over the years, but she is still depicted with three heads and is supposed to be able to see into the past as well as the future. She was sometimes called the Goddess of the Crossroads and was reputed to have the power to create or withhold storms. As a result, she became the goddess of shepherds and sailors. Jean Shinoda Bolen, author of *Goddesses in Older Women*, calls her the Goddess of Intuition and suggests, "You must listen to what she says in the voice of your own intuition." In the years before satellite-assisted weather forecasting, the small-boat skipper was forced to use intuition as well as experience when deciding whether it was safe to make the crossing or not. At times even the great Haida canoes broke up in unexpected storms. I had no prior experience in this part of the coast, and no satellite information, but I felt deep in my gut that everything was going to be all right, and it was.

After we navigated the shoals and broke free into the approach to Skidegate Inlet, we were able to look around. The shallow foreshore was surrounded by low hills. Unlike on the mainland, there appeared to be no high mountains. To our right was a scattering of houses and a few larger structures that we assumed to be the Native settlement of Skidegate; just past it were about a dozen nondescript buildings. So this was the fabled "City," our goal after 14 hours en route?

Although the town was small, the expansive docking facilities were unexpectedly generous. We were able to find a good tie-up spot on the inside at the end of a finger. This not only gave us protection from the slop of boats coming and going, but also gave us privacy at our back door. Our first job was to put on the deck cover because we could see rain clouds coming over nearby hills. We were soon to learn that it rained a bit every day. No wonder people called these the Misty Isles.

We had only snacked all day, so dinner was at the top of our list of things to do. After a quick wash-up, we found our way to the ramp and stepped ashore. The land was heaving gently, as it always does after a stint at sea. We turned left and soon spotted a lively game of baseball at the nearby athletic field. A team of sturdy Native fellows was hard at it, playing against a mixed team of mostly White guys. Everybody seemed to be having fun. We turned left, found the ubiquitous Chinese restaurant and settled happily into a booth. Within minutes the whole baseball crowd tumbled through the doorway and kept the lone waitress busy serving up coffee, Coke and stir-fry. It was just as well that we were too tired to talk, because the noise level soared. But it was good to be surrounded by such a happy crowd. We knew right then that we were going to enjoy these islands.

It was still daylight when we left the café after nine o'clock, so we went for a stroll along the beach. We were delighted to find numerous shellfish fossils studding the sandstone bank. In places they were as far up as my shoulder. This told me that the ocean must have been even higher at one time, or the land much lower. Of course, we filled our pockets. But if you asked me today to see those treasures that I gathered, I wouldn't know where to find them. Instead of doing the archeologically correct thing and leaving them right where they were, we naively carried them back to the boat.

Next morning, two young loggers came down for a chat. They worked at a small camp in an inlet on the outside of Moresby Island, but were in town for a five-day break. One fellow, Will Rodd, had a small Suzuki Jeep and offered to take us over to the Native band office at Skidegate when it opened on Monday so that we could get our permit for landing at old Haida village sites. White settlers had never signed a treaty with the local indigenous people, and by 1983 the Haida were chafing at their lack of control of ancestral lands. The permits were the opening salvo in what eventually became a land claim. If we were to visit Ninstints on Anthony Island at the lower end of Moresby Island, we certainly wanted a permit on board.

At Queen Charlotte City, Paul and June met Will Rodd, who took them to see the sights on Graham Island. Here, Paul works on making a repair to *Wood Duck* while Will looks on.

Will proved to be a gem. He said that since we all had a Sunday to spend, he would take us to see the sights on Graham Island. We crammed ourselves into his snug two-person Jeep. I sat on a folded jacket that covered the gearbox/handbrake assembly, with my feet crowded in beside Paul's. I had to crouch down because my head brushed against the canvas roof, but it sure beat walking the distance. We went to see the golden spruce. This unique and glorious tree stood across a creek from us, a glowing shaft of sunlight amidst the dense green of the forest. A few years later Grant Hadwin, a misguided fellow who wanted to draw attention to the horrors of clear-cutting, killed it. He saw immense irony in the fact that no one was revering all the other huge old-growth trees that were being logged at an astounding rate, so he felled the only known golden spruce in existence, never stopping to think that he was destroying a Haida icon. In his book *The Golden Spruce*, John Vaillant tells the story of the tree and of Hadwin, who apparently drowned when he later escaped to the sea in his small kayak.

We were fortunate to visit this beauty while it still lived. After letting us fill our eyes and our cameras, Will took us tramping through the woods to see a large, partially finished dugout canoe. I was a bit skeptical at first because I didn't realize that Haida canoe builders always chose the perfect tree (even if it stood some distance from the ocean), cut away most of the unwanted wood and then slid the giant to the water on rollers. That made a lot more sense than trying to haul a complete log to the water by hand. And good trees grow where they feel like growing, not where you would choose them to be.

What amazed me about this partially shaped canoe was its size. I could not understand how the workers could fall a tree of suitable diameter for boat building. It was not until I read Hilary Stewart's book *Cedar* that I began to understand how they tackled this problem. Mature cedar trees have huge buttressing supports at the base that are related to the root formation. The trunk does not even out for many feet above the ground. A wise logger will usually make his first cut at this height. But now he can no longer stand on the ground. Much like the high-riggers in modern day logging, the Native faller employed a support system so that his first cut was well up the tree. Using cedar withes, the slender "branchlets that hang down from the main branches in long, graceful curves," he fashioned supports for his body and for his feet. The back support was woven of split cedar withes, with a three-ply withe rope that went around the tree trunk, while the footrest was formed of a curved section of plank, often shaped like a fish. It had holes at both ends, with one end held by a large knot, while the other consisted of a slipknot for easy adjustment according to the circumference of the tree being felled. The withes had a breaking strength of 425 pounds and so were up to the task.

As to tools for cutting such a massive tree, the Haida fashioned cutting blades out of hard stone such as jade. This particular material can be shaped to form an amazingly sharp edge. The Natives would also have had metal tools even before Europeans arrived in the Queen Charlottes, garnered from their astute trading with other First Nations up and down the coast and from the wrecks of Asian ships that washed up on the beaches of Graham Island because of its proximity to the Japanese current.

Once the roughed-out canoe had been manhandled through the forest, it was set up on the beach in front of the longhouses, where artisans began the laborious task of whittling away any excess wood and shaping the outside. When the hull was ready (although it was still log-shaped), fires were built nearby, and the inside of the canoe was filled with water. Stones heated till they were red-hot were lifted into this water, which actually came to a boil, softening the wood. At the right time, canoe builders stretched the opening wider with their hands, inserted braces between the sides and, voila, a canoe was born!

This abandoned log was meant to be carved into a canoe, but it split before the process was completed. The Haida would cut away most of the unwanted wood while a log was still in the forest before they skidded it to the beach.

The intricately carved tall bow and the stern were applied after the hull was the right shape. The final task was to scorch the vessel to help preserve it from rot. This treatment would help the canoe slide smoothly through the water and also discourage insects from taking a bite; it could be repeated whenever necessary. Even today, people with wooden hulls use this technique to kill off borers without having to dig them out of the wood.

I was pleased to learn that northern Natives used sails, made of fabric woven from red-cedar bark, long before they saw the Europeans' huge ships. Running before the wind under sail certainly beat paddling the distance to and from the mainland. They would often wait days for a suitable tailwind to help them on their way. When it arrived, the sails were fastened to poles that reached out like bat wings on either side of the hull.

Haida canoes had long been a major trading item on the nearby mainland. Groups of new ones were paddled across Hecate Strait to be exchanged for goods or slaves, leaving the Haida with no option but to use their old decrepit canoes to ferry crew and cargo back to the islands. The canoes' lack of ribs meant that, in rough weather, fragile hulls sometimes split lengthwise, dumping crew and passengers into the briny, so travelling in a flotilla made a lot of sense. Even so, I am sure a number of lives were lost when unexpected storms hit during the trip home.

The roughed-out log we saw in the woods was going nowhere, so we shoehorned ourselves back into the Jeep, and Will drove on toward New Masset. The appearance of a motley collection of houses told us we were getting near. Neither Paul nor I asked to see the town, so Will veered off to the right and drove us toward the beach. I would have dearly liked to see the original Native village that was closer to the mouth of the inlet but felt that would be an imposition on our driver and on the Native people who lived there. Also, it was unlikely that anything remained of the old longhouses and totems after so many years of contact with White people's ways.

It was at this village, Old Masset, that the seeds of Christianity were sown amongst the Haida. By the early 19th century, disease and alcohol had so decimated tribes all up and down the coast that they were in disarray. In 1860, Methodist missionaries came to the north coast and brought some measure of health and order to the Native people, especially the Tsimshians near Port Simpson. Although many tribal customs had been discouraged by these dedicated Victorians, enough good had come out of their efforts that forward-looking Native leaders began to realize there was no turning back the clock.

The first chief to show an interest was a young man by the name of Seegay, whose wife could speak both Haida and Tsimshian languages. The couple was introduced to Rev. William Collison, who had come to the mission at Metlakatla on the mainland with his wife in 1873. Collison set to work learning the Tsimshian language, and by the time he met Seegay in 1875, he was quite proficient. Seegay invited him to come to Masset. In June 1876, Collison set out by canoe with some Haidas to make the hazardous crossing. He arrived at Masset to find that the other chiefs lacked Seegay's enthusiasm. However, they did permit the minister to speak to the men assembled in Chief Weah's longhouse. The outcome of this speech was that Weah gave Collison permission to teach the children. On the strength of this promise, Collison came back in September on the Hudson's Bay Company steamer *Otter*, bringing along his wife and their two baby daughters. Collison's wife's courage obviously matched that of her husband.

According to Florence Edenshaw Davidson, who spent all her life (1896–1993) at Masset, the church flourished in spite of the chiefs' initial resistance. One of her ancestors, Chief Edenshaw, certainly did not want missionaries on the island. He had many, many slaves, and he knew that the clergy frowned upon slavery. But in 1885 Florence's parents, who had been married in a Haida ceremony 12 years earlier, were married in the church at Masset. Her father, Charles Edenshaw, became one of the most famous Native carvers of all time. At 15 years of age, Florence entered into an arranged marriage with Robert Davidson, who also spent his long life carving for collectors and museums worldwide. As Florence told her biographer, Margaret B. Blackman, girls had no choice in the matter. Marriages formed important liaisons and were often planned years in advance.

Both her father and her husband supported their families with the art they produced. Certainly Davidson had his work cut out for him in this regard, because he and Florence had 13 children. One of the most popular items they made for sale was silver jewellery. When my aunt and uncle were salmon fishing near Masset, Aunt Bettie gave Davidson some silver dollars, and he turned them into a handsome bracelet decorated with totem-like figures. According to Florence, Edenshaw used the scraps of silver to make small items like earrings for his pretty daughter.

Florence remained involved with the church through her own long life. She reported that activities in the church were an adjunct to many of the traditional Haida social events, although activities like the potlatch went underground, and puberty rites for girls vanished entirely. Among the Natives' many adaptations in response to church edicts was the switch to making button blankets part of the Native ritual dress, because the church actively discouraged the carving of huge totem poles. Carvers began drawing their designs on blankets, and women stitched white buttons along the outline. Now they could wear their crest instead of displaying their lineage on a pole.

It seems to me that the Haida are astute business people who have learned to adapt as times change. They saw the market for trinkets and small art forms, so they responded by churning out quantities of fine, portable items. They also saw the devastation of the land and the huge profits earned by international logging companies. They mourned the subsequent decline in salmon stocks and decided to reassert their control over these islands. This stirring of pride, with its renewed sense of direction, was in its infancy when Paul and I visited in 1983. What we saw then and what is now are worlds apart, but still, I'm sorry I missed visiting Florence's village.

Will turned off the road to Masset and took a route that got more and more primitive as we went east. It led us toward Tow Hill, a sharp volcanic intrusion that rises some 200 feet above the sand and is visible from the sea. He pulled his little vehicle up near the beach, and we unwedged ourselves. I am sure we all had creases from where we were pressed together in his little car. I grabbed the picnic container from the back, and we strolled out onto a glorious sandy beach, picked out a weather-beaten log and settled down to a welcome bit of lunch, gazing out over the gently undulating swells that tumbled and hissed up on the shore.

After a quiet, contemplative interval, Will began to talk. He told us this place had become his sanctuary. He came here after working in North Africa, drilling oil wells. The job had been so stressful that it threatened his health, so he decided to go somewhere

Will Rodd on North Beach, Graham Island. This is where Haida mythology says life began after the flood. It is also where Will recovered his health after working in the oil industry in North Africa.

remote, camp out and try to recover his health. He flew home to Nova Scotia, visited his family for a few weeks, bought his Jeep, loaded in a tent and minimal camping gear and filled up all the remaining space with magazines and books. He decided he'd drive as far west as he could and still stay in Canada. Along the way he studied the maps and decided that the remotest spot was at the tip of the Queen Charlotte Islands. His journey ended on the beach where we sat. "I set up my tent, gathered some stones and built a firepit, boiled up a good old Nova Scotia stewpot, ate till I was full, climbed into my sleeping bag and fell blissfully asleep. I became a primitive, read and hiked, explored the sandspit to the end and spent the whole winter camping with nothing but the seabirds, waves and wind for company. By the end of that year I felt alive again, so I thought I'd do something different. I went logging."

Indeed it was a healing, magical spot. Haida mythology says life began here after the flood. It was on this stretch of sand that Raven found the giant clamshell containing tiny creatures that emerged to form the nucleus of all living things. The myth of the shell inspired Bill Reid's wondrous sculpture that brings such delight to those who see it today.

In 1983, we were the only humans there. We strolled along, picking up countless shining agates near a large stream and breathing in the cool salty air while seabirds soared above us in the updrafts. A mist hid Alaska from our view, so we could not see the land where Haida had also lived for years. It seemed as though we had reached the end of the earth, with nothing in view but the ever-rolling sea.

11 SKIDEGATE NARROWS

Both Paul and I were determined to explore as much of the outer coastline as possible with the remaining days left to us before we had to head back home. The best way to do this was to venture through Skidegate Narrows, the narrow gap that separates Graham Island to the north from Moresby Island to the south. We wanted to visit Anthony Island, at the far end of Moresby, and I had charts for the entire trip, although some of the details were vague. There were places that were totally devoid of soundings, but I figured that with care, our slow speed and our habit of maintaining a visual lookout, we would survive. Neither of us could be called hypercautious when it came to nautical matters, but there was no point in travelling all this distance and not tasting the joy of exploring new waterways or discovering new places.

Back in Queen Charlotte City, I noticed that Will's friend, a prawn fisherman, had returned to his boat, so I asked him about navigating Skidegate Narrows. He was horrified and assured me that we didn't want to go there. That news took me by surprise, so I rowed back to check out our charts. A close look at the one for Skidegate Channel was enough to give me the golly-wobbles. We were planning to go through THERE! In places there was almost no water at low tide, and much of the east narrows had less than five feet of water at those times. Our boat required at least six feet of clearance because of the deep keel.

Years later I asked my cousin Rod if he had ever gone through those narrows. He chuckled and said that his first time was the worst time. The salmon trollers had heard that a run of tuna had swept within five miles of the outer coast, so the fishermen changed their gear and went chasing after these fast-swimming beauties. Rod had a load of salmon on board, so he hurried over to Prince Rupert, unloaded his catch and re-rigged his 46-foot troller, the *Valiant I*. After a round of frantic work that included refuelling and reprovisioning, he and his two crew members headed back across Hecate Strait.

When he got to Queen Charlotte City, most of the fishing boats had already left port. His friend Ed Hansen of the *Galley Bay* was still there, so they travelled together. Neither of them had tackled Skidegate Narrows before, and going with a buddy who could haul you free if you went aground made the challenge safer. They passed some fishboats caught in the mud on either side of that ghastly passageway, so he and Ed navigated slowly, keeping to places where no one was stuck, and managed to get through the narrows unscathed.

It was obvious that I needed help with this navigational challenge. So I rolled up the chart and took it along with me while I went for a walk along the floats. There was bound to be someone who was familiar with the route. Sure enough, not two floats away I spotted a fisherman who was repairing gear on the back deck of a substantial troller. He said that he preferred to fish the west coast so went through the narrows on a regular basis. We spread out the chart on top of the fish hold and he took me through the route. He held the chart upside down and printed his instructions on it with his own version of spelling—he certainly knew his navigation, even if his schoolteachers might have despaired. He told me to use the tide tables for Hecate Strait. There had to be at least 11 feet of water above datum before I could even consider the trip. Also, I needed to go on a rising tide. Strangely, the current always flows in one direction, from east to west, but it is stronger on a falling tide, so if we followed his instructions we would be swept along less quickly.

Painstaking instructions printed right on the chart give depths of water along the route compared to the depth at Queen Charlotte City. This helped me understand why my mentor required 11 feet of water as a minimum before we even ventured out. According to the chart, when there was 23 feet of water at the city there would be 19 at the mid-beacon, 13.5 at the west beacon and 12 in the west narrows. I calculated that would give us about 2.5 feet of water over the shallowest spot if we arrived there when there was only 11 feet at the city. Possibly my informant did not need as much depth with his keel. But, based on his calculations, if we left on a rising tide there would be sufficient water by the time we reached the shallowest place. I began to understand the prawn man's apprehension, but I was also grateful for the salmon fisherman's input.

He said, "I'm heading through a little after lunch tomorrow. You guys will be going a lot slower than me, so if you start out at about noon, I'll catch up to you and then you can follow me through."

I thanked him profusely. That arrangement would leave us time to go to the band office in the morning and then pick up a few fresh groceries before we got underway.

Monday morning came with the usual showers, but they cleared up by the time Will arrived to take us to Skidegate for our landing permit. We squeezed into his sardine can and went along the road past houses, shoreline installations and small businesses until we reached the outskirts of the Native village. Near the band office, several totem poles lay across wooden supports to keep them up off the grass. We took some photographs, but I was too apprehensive about the upcoming navigational challenge to want to linger. We had no trouble getting our legal papers. Then Will loaded us back in the vehicle and took us to the grocery store. I remember nothing about the store itself, but I think I could paint a portrait of the handsome Haida women who were there; they were so impressive, laughing and chatting as they waited for the clerk to process their grocery orders. There was nothing tiny or timid about any of them. They were tall and solid looking with curly, shining black hair and silver jewellery.

Near the band office at Skidegate, totem poles awaiting repair lay across wooden supports.

I am not alone in making this observation about the Haida. In *Ghostland People*, Charles Lillard quotes John Schouler, Hudson's Bay Company surgeon and naturalist, who observed, "The Charlotte islanders as specimens, are far the best looking, most energetic people of the N.W. Coast." Schouler went on to report that they did not bind the heads of infants to flatten them, but the women used the labret in their lower lip. The women we saw were too modern to use a lip ornament that would stretch the bottom lip out of shape, but they certainly fitted Schouler's description otherwise.

Will took us back to the dock and reminded us of our promise to drop by the small logging camp where he worked at Englefield Bay on the outer coast of Moresby Island. He helped cast off our lines and stood watching from the end of the float as we putted off toward our big adventure. Paul tootled our horn, we waved goodbye, and I clutched the chart, because the navigational challenges began just a mile away when we rounded Lina Island. Of course, the fisherman had indicated the shortest route, and that meant rock dodging, but that was what the trip was all about. We needed to stick to his instructions if we were to meet him farther along our route.

We were just approaching the east narrows when he zoomed past us with a wave of his hand out the pilothouse window. He was going fishing and was in a hurry. I am sure he had no idea that four and a half knots was our top speed, and in no time he was out of sight. So much for guiding us through the passageway. At least he had marked our charts. I could feel my heart rate go up, but I hid this from Paul. He had utter confidence in my navigational skills, and I wasn't about to let him down.

There were beacons everywhere. The old-time Haida would have had a good laugh at all of these innovations, but the sight of them certainly gladdened my heart. We could see mud flats under the clear water on either side of us and were grateful that there was no spawn. There are times when the ocean is almost opaque with spawn from barnacles and other such creatures. The mud below us was so soft that any response from our echo sounder would be vague, and I was sure that in a grounding we would mush right into it and stick firmly.

Just as we neared the shore and put in a sharp turn to our right, we spotted a tug with a barge coming toward us. I put my hand over my eyes and waved to the skipper, who pulled to one side and slowed down. We could see him grinning through the windshield as we passed close by in a channel that I swear was only 30 feet wide. At the west beacon we reached a whirlpool area, so we took the fisherman's advice: goose it. Paul gunned the motor and we zoomed right through. To my great relief there was no sign of a major whirlpool anywhere.

The passageway opened up, and then Trounce Inlet appeared to our right. Now we faced the most nerve-wracking part of the trip as we entered west narrows, which seemed to sprawl out on either side of us. Mud flats, visible underwater, abounded everywhere. Paul throttled right back and I hung over the bow, but a westerly breeze had built up ripples and it was hard to gauge the depth. I was mighty glad that I had spent my younger years fishing from a rowboat, because it had given me some practice in the difficult art of separating surface reflections from objects that are under the water. As it was, we went too far to starboard. I gasped in horror when I spotted clamshells right below us, where a creek had made an underwater channel through the mud bottom. Had we gone any farther in that direction, we might have grounded.

After working past that hazard, we were able to make a turn to port. The final section was near the shore, and soon we were in the clear. Although we had only travelled about 15 miles that day, they were the longest, most stressful miles I had ever gone. My tense shoulder muscles gradually relaxed, and I turned to smile at Paul. I could tell by his grin that I hadn't fooled him for a minute. We had both been scared.

12 THE WEST COAST AT LAST

Chaatl Island is a square block that sits to the left of the exit from the narrows. On the chart it looks like a chunk some giant chopped loose from Anthony Island, then forgot to push back into place. There is a water passageway on two sides, with mooring buoys thoughtfully provided in the nearest arm, so we tied up gratefully for our first night on the outer coast of the Charlottes. There was a long-abandoned Native village somewhere along the nearby channel, but getting to it with our heavy rowboat and just a pair of oars would require more energy than either of us was prepared to expend. We were indeed lazy pikers, because in 1912 Emily Carr had found her way to what she called Cha-atl Island so that she could make sketches of the handsome totem poles that soared up to the heavens behind the battered old longhouse surrounded by brush and deep grass.

She was 41 years old, no doubt dressed in the typical long skirts and high, leather, button boots of the day, with a hat clamped firmly on her head and a fierce determination to record the powerful examples of Native sculpture that remained on this coast. She was a contemporary of my maternal grandmother, who by that time had nine children and was just trying to get through each day without collapsing. By rejecting marriage and the complications of motherhood, Emily was pursuing her dream—and putting up with unimaginable discomfort in the process.

In *Seven Journeys*, Doris Shadbolt describes how Emily hired a Native with a canoe and brought her sketchbooks, a carpetbag and probably her dog. Although the village had been abandoned for some years, there were still 21 houses there when Dr. Charles Newcombe photographed it in 1903. In his photo, a dozen or more totem poles are still standing, although some lean forward precariously. In one of Emily's finished paintings of Chaatl, the longhouse has moss on the roof, along with a small tree. The gable sags and there is a blank doorway. Behind the house stand three complex totem poles, each one representing the history of a different chief, with the bands at the top showing the number of potlatches given by that particular august personage. The potlatch was not an occasion to be taken lightly, for the celebration was expensive beyond belief. Emily may not have been aware of the significance of these rings, but historians should be grateful for her careful depiction of these monuments because most of them are now long gone.

Given the fact that it rains nearly every day on these islands, I can easily imagine the discomfort the artist endured. By late day she would long for dry heat and hot food. I hope that her guide met these needs and was able to build up a good fire in one of the remaining houses, where she could sit on a log and sort through her day's work.

On this trip she spent six weeks travelling the BC coast, venturing into the Skeena River valley and across to the Queen Charlotte Islands, visiting village sites, filling her sketchbooks with images of an art form that was fast disappearing from view, rotting away in the underbrush. Aside from astute collectors for various museums, Emily was one of the few people who recognized that the creative majesty of Native carvings was equal to that of revered sculptures produced anywhere in the world, especially given the tools used.

After spending a year studying art in Paris, Emily had changed her style of painting to reflect the impressionist movement that was struggling for acceptance in Europe. This new style was more appropriate for the wildness of the coast, which demanded a looser technique than was in vogue in BC at the time. She must have painted like a maniac after her trip, because she held a solo exhibition of

200 works in Vancouver the following year. Unfortunately, her sales were dismally disappointing. She went home to Victoria and did almost no painting for about 11 years. My father told me that in the 1930s, one of the schools where he taught paid her $50 for a painting; in 2006, an Emily Carr painting of a single pole at Chaatl sold for nearly half a million dollars.

But here we were, 70 years after her visit, all snug aboard our little sailboat with the wood-burning stove wafting aromatic smoke, and the awning overhead keeping out raindrops. Had we more time and a strong inflatable, we would have gone to see if anything remained of Chaatl village, but we were tired from our challenging squirm through Skidegate Narrows and ready for a quiet evening on board. Although we lacked a Native guide who could find local food treats, we knew that with a little effort and our small rowboat we would never go hungry, so we went looking to see what this sheltered spot had to offer.

The bottom of the sea was alive with rock crabs. These vicious, hard-shelled cousins of the Dungeness are real scrappers. You just have to lower a stick in front of them and they attack it. In no time we had five or six cranky fellows scrabbling around in the bilge. Our visit to the grocery store earlier in the day had yielded buns and salad stuff, so we were all set: hot crab tonight and crab sandwiches tomorrow.

During the evening I studied the charts and tried to figure out our next move. It was nearing the end of July. We had to spend our time wisely, leaving room in our schedule for foul weather. Our small craft was safe as long as we did not hurry. If the gentle winds continued, we could spend a few days exploring the coast of Graham Island before turning to work our way down toward Anthony Island at the southern end of the archipelago.

Over the years, cousin Rod had told me many stories about the Charlottes that whetted my appetite for exploration, even though I knew Rod's courage and devil-may-care attitude, backed by his wiry strength, led him into adventures far beyond what I would want. In the 1950s he fished for salmon along the outer shores of both large islands. Usually he had a helper, but one year he fished alone. After spending the night at a fishing camp on the north end of Graham Island, he decided to try his luck trolling near Shag Rock in the direction of Virago Sound. It was calm with a pea-soup fog (unusual for that area), and no fish were interested in his lures, so he switched on the automatic pilot and was putting along, half-asleep, when he happened to glance at the depth sounder. The bottom was coming right up at him! He threw the clutch into reverse, because he thought he was running onto Shag Rock. How had he become so lost?

Suddenly a huge whale surfaced in front of him, right between the bow poles, and exhaled a great mist of air. Both he and the whale had been caught snoozing. Rod's wry comment in his letter was that a whale's breath leaves something to be desired. Luckily for Rod, the whale was too sleepy to be cranky when it was disturbed.

During another lull in fishing, Rod left his boat tucked in a safe harbour in Parry Passage, between Langara and Graham islands, and hiked with a buddy as far south as they could go along the west coast. On the first beach they spotted a half-buried Second World War mine. It was round, with tube-like projections all over the outside. He couldn't resist taking a shot at it with his rifle. Fortunately, it didn't blow up or he'd still be flying. (When I read Kathleen Dalzell's outstanding book *The Queen Charlotte Islands, Vol. 2*, a few years later, I learned that the navy eventually detonated the mine, creating a huge explosion and an equally astonishing hole in the sand. It is just as well Rod's bullet missed a sensitive point.)

As he and his friend hiked farther south, they discovered a path well above the beach. The Haida called it the Bear Trail because in years past they had set bear traps along the way. They had also used this route to get to their sea otter camps along the coast. Rod said that it was rugged going. At one point Rod and his pal finally got down to the shore and walked right through a high outcropping that led from one beach to the next. This long passageway amounted to a split in the solid rock, with walls on either side that rose some 300 to 500 feet. Rod figured an earthquake must have caused it. There were smoke stains and red ochre markings on the lower walls.

Sometimes the trail ran along the tops of these outcroppings, but wherever they did find a gap, they scrambled down to walk in the sand. Although they could carry nothing back with them, Rod said it was worth the effort to make the descent. Among the hordes of glass balls that had drifted over from Japanese fishing nets there were some floats shaped like rolling pins, several feet long, with knobs on the ends. Wild bamboo had taken root high up on the shoreline. The two men also spotted the bones of a huge whale with a bent harpoon still tangled amongst the ribs. The vertebrae were big enough to use as seats. Rod hauled a few of those up into the woods, hoping that he could come back later to fetch them. A few steps farther along was a fossilized clam that was as wide as a garbage can lid.

At one point in their hike they came upon the remains of a Chinese junk that had been constructed of large, hand-adzed hardwood planks. Blade marks were still visible on the inner surfaces. The timbers were up to 10 inches thick and had been bleached by the sun. The original dowel fastenings still held the wood together, with not a scrap of metal in the whole construction.

Wind-driven objects like glass float-balls for fishing nets are commonly found all down the Pacific shoreline, but the beaches near the northern tip of the Charlottes gather a much wider variety of items. Woolly things, like coconuts, usually sport a hefty beard of gooseneck barnacles that slow them down and prevent the wind from skipping them along the surface. Rod said that the Japanese current occasionally sweeps close inshore, and the crescent-shaped projections of sandy beaches act as gentler traps than much of this rock-strewn coast. With Rod's stories filling my ears, is it any wonder I longed to see the area that he had explored, in spite of the challenge of getting there from our sheltered anchorage at Chaatl Island?

We woke to a sunny morning. After casting off from the mooring buoy at nine, we soon found ourselves in a gentle outflow wind from Skidegate Channel, so we rolled out the genoa to accompany the mainsail, which would remain up most of the time we were travelling. Since we were gliding along nicely at three and a half knots, Paul suggested we try a spot of west coast fishing. Within minutes he landed a 10-pound spring salmon, and I caught a pink, because I had left the black-spotted hot pink lure on my line from our last trolling enterprise. This lure is far more attractive to pinks than it is to the bigger fish. I took over the helm and Paul set to work gutting and filleting the fish. I wrapped them in newspaper, slipped them inside a plastic bag and stored it next to the skin of the boat under the settee. The fish would stay cool there until I could salt them down in the evening.

As the breeze died away, we set our course to sail past the outer side of Marble Island. By noon we were moving with the engine ticking over at the usual four and a half knots. Except for the great swells, there were no waves, so we sat on the back deck, munching snacks and marvelling at the colour of the breakers as they rumbled up onto the shore or crashed with a mighty roar on isolated rocks. In the sunshine the foam was stark white, exposing the most amazing turquoise underneath. Below our hull, between the streaks of foam, the ocean was endlessly clear. I remembered my brother, George, telling me that when he fished off the coast of Vancouver Island he could always tell when he reached the northward-flowing Japanese current because the water became ever so blue and warm. Maybe we were in that flow as well. After all, this was an El Niño year, with strange creatures venturing farther up the coast than usual.

By four o'clock in the afternoon, we were tied to one of the mooring buoys behind Cadman Island in Kano Inlet. Paul would have preferred to swing at anchor, but I had read Kathleen Dalzell's account of this area in *The Queen Charlotte Islands, Vol. 2.* She said that in stormy conditions, wind and waves roar through the gap between the small island and the shore with enough force to dislodge anything in their path. This information certainly encouraged us to use the moorages offered, because we would be stuck here until the fish-smoking project was finished, and who knew what the weather might be like out on this exposed coastline?

Our first walk on the west coast of the Charlottes that afternoon was in unspoiled wilderness. Aside from the mooring buoys, there was no sign that the hand of human progress had reached this treasured spot. When we ventured into the forest, I finally understood what Longfellow meant when he wrote about Native people moving silently through the woods as they stalked deer. As a youthful reader, I always scoffed at that description. I had grown up on the lower coast, where logging and attempts by the pioneers to clear away the forest had encouraged the plentiful growth of salal and other bushes. "Stalkers" literally snapped and rustled as they forced their way through the rampant undergrowth. A deer would have to be stone deaf not to hear the approach.

Here, however, our noiseless footsteps sank into a bottomless carpet of moss. Old trees that had finally collapsed were rounded lumps that provided variety in an otherwise gently undulating surface. Even in the fading light of the day, it was almost as dark as night, with tree branches forming a freckled ceiling over our heads. We came to a halt, completely mesmerized by our surroundings. Columns of tree trunks sheathed in mottled green velvet rose on all sides. Our voices diminished to whispers.

We had not been expecting this glorious experience when we rowed ashore. At first we had scrounged the shoreline looking for old knots to burn in our stove. After finding a few, we had wandered into the woods, remembering Bill Killam's suggestion that fallen trees had projecting knobs on them that would also make excellent firewood. Our ramble yielded a few, which I tucked into a plastic carryall, but our greatest need at the moment was some hardwood for the fish smoker.

Paul had brought his folding pruning saw so he could gather branches of green alder to provide smoke, but the only deciduous trees to be found were at the fringes of the woods, where they reached pleading arms out in search of sunshine. Instead of being tall and generous trees, these were mere bushes that had been trimmed for years by the teeth of small resident deer. I thought they resembled the vine maples that grow so prolifically in the lower Fraser Valley. We found out much later that they were Sitka alder, which never grows to the size of the red alder that abounds on the lower BC coast.

It was sunny by the time we arose that first morning behind Cadman Island. While Paul cleaned up the galley after breakfast, I rinsed the loose salt off the salmon slices and spread them out on newspaper on the back deck. Then I poked my head into the cabin and said, "Hey, Paul, I think I'll go for a row to the beach and see if the low tide has exposed any more knots. You'll be busy assembling that new metal smoker, and I'll only be in the way. See you in a while." As part of a team, I rarely got to do the rowing, which I loved, so it was a bit of a holiday for me to go off alone. And he needed time to fit together all the pieces of his creation. The first year that we smoked fish on board, we used a clumsy wooden affair that did the job but took up precious space under the back deck when it was not in use, so ingenious Paul had designed a knockdown metal unit with sides that slid together. He had crimped the long edges and welded supports inside to hold three wire shelves. There was a drip tray at the bottom to catch the greasy juices that always managed to escape from the meat. Testing time was near.

When I got to the beach, I found it pocked with empty seashells and more knots for the fire. Since I was in no hurry to return to the boat, I wandered along saying over and over, "Thank you, God, for guiding me here. This is so beautiful." There was no heaped tangle of discarded logs, no garbage cluttering the beach, no rumble of machinery and, except for the hiss of the wavelets as they reached the shore, all was quiet and virginal . . . until I came upon a steaming pile of bear scat. Oh dear! The boat suddenly looked very good to me. I didn't want to appear afraid, so I ambled off in the direction of the rowboat and slowly pulled it back down into the water. Once I had the oars in my hands, I rowed like an Olympic champion.

Paul chuckled when I told him about my adventure. And after I scrambled up onto the deck, I admired his creation. "Oh, Paul, that looks just great. You have it anchored so snugly to the handrails that it'll withstand just about any knocking about by wind or waves. Congratulations!"

"Now let's see if it does the job," he replied. After sliding the loaded shelves into place, he went below to feed green alder chunks

The second smoker that Paul designed was a knockdown metal unit with sides that slid together. Three wire shelves inside held the fish, and a drip tray at the bottom caught the greasy juices. The smoker sat on the cabin roof and wafted the delicious scent of smoked salmon toward the nearby seine boats that were tied to another mooring buoy.

into the stove. When the chimney began to issue a goodly plume of smoke, he plugged the top of the stack with a wrap of aluminum foil, and the smoke began oozing out around the top edges of the box. It worked! By the afternoon we were sipping a glass of wine, and our chins were smeared with tasty juice from sampling the contents of his invention.

When 12 seine boats and one Fisheries and Oceans Canada vessel roared into the harbour, we felt very much in the way. I am sure the fishermen were surprised to find a small wooden sailboat snugly tied to one of the Fisheries' buoys, but no one made any comment, so we waved and stayed put. One of the smaller seine boats off-loaded its fish to a packer, which left in a roar of engines. Around us, crew members set to work doing repairs and washing down the decks. Then all was quiet. With the dawn came a great rumbling of diesel engines as the boats pulled out to sea, leaving us alone in the great grey stillness, waiting for the birdsong to resume.

13 TELLING STORIES

The gentle wind that had teased the aromatic smoke during the long day began to strum the rigging with serious intent. Given our shortage of time, this was not good news. "Oh bother," I sighed. "By the sound of things, we are not going anywhere tomorrow. I've been looking at the charts and there are great stretches of unsurveyed water ahead of us with little shelter along the way. I know we'll be okay if we can just take our time and go slowly in gentle weather with the swells to guide us, but we'd better head back in the direction of Moresby Island. Rod's wonderful beaches will have to manage without our footprints in the sand. For now, we'll be like the Natives in earlier days and settle down around the fire, telling stories, until the wind lets up."

"Sounds good to me, June. What do you have on the shelf? Any Indian ones?"

"As a matter of fact, I have. I brought along George Clutesi's great fable collection, *Son of Raven, Son of Deer*."

George Clutesi was born on the west coast of Vancouver Island in 1905. He drew and painted as a child, and when he returned to his art in the 1940s, he became a protegé of Emily Carr, painting portraits. That is a thin living at best, and he had a family to feed, so he was chasing salmon in the summertime. He met and became friends with my brother, who had my high school graduation photo pinned up in the wheelhouse of his fishboat. When Clutesi saw it, he said he'd like to do my portrait, so that fall he came to my parents' house in Vancouver. He was a fine-looking, pleasant, soft-spoken man who came with his sketchbook and charcoal to do the initial study.

His portrait showed all my structural faults. I have a crooked face and do not notice it when I look in a mirror, but when it was presented to me in reverse image (which is what you get with a portrait), I was stunned. Nothing ever came of the project. I assume my brother paid him for his time. I certainly hope so. This is obviously one of the hazards for the portraitist: everyone likes the result except the one who is depicted, because others see a face from the same point of view as the artist.

I did not hear of Clutesi for another 29 years. In the meantime, he began doing art that reflected his ancestry. He also wrote his wonderful collection of fables from his childhood and illustrated them with delightful pen-and-ink drawings of the creatures in the stories. At one time the Department of Education purchased enough copies that every grade five child in the province had one to read and study. Native elders went into the schools with their traditional masks and did mini-plays, with the children acting out the roles. This was much the same way George remembered learning the stories himself as his nana taught him about his role in relation to nature and mankind. George's tales remind me of Aesop's fables, which reflect a similar culture on the other side of the world.

I met Clutesi again when he was the keynote speaker at a convention of English teachers from all across Canada. The group filled all the chairs in the ballroom at the Hotel Vancouver. George arrived carrying a carved wand that he called his "talking stick." He told us that his father and grandfather had both been the official speakers, whose responsibility was to remember all the history of their tribe. When they were holding the "talking stick," they also held the floor in a gathering. This honour went from father to son. He told us about his childhood at home and about being taken away to the residential school at Alberni when he was six years old. He was so unhappy that he would sneak into his older sister's bed at night so she could comfort him. Then he talked about his youth and what it was like in the longhouse when the speaker's voice filled the air on a stormy winter night. We sat there totally mesmerized while his voice thundered and roared like the wind, then softened like waves sizzling back down a pebbled beach. When he stopped speaking, no one moved while the quivering shadows of that voice hung in the air. Then we all surged to our feet, clapping and roaring our approval. Here was a Native man showing teachers of English the power of the spoken word. Tears streamed down our faces at the wonder of it all.

Years later, the strength of that amazing voice and the quality of the man carried the movie *Dreamspeaker*, in which he played the role of an old First Nations man who helped a troubled boy cope with the demons that tormented him and drove him to destroy his surroundings.

I saw that film a second time when I was a 52-year-old student at the Western Washington University. One of the professors spoke of it in a lecture about using the power of fable when working with children—Clutesi's character told the story of Sisiutl when he was dealing with the boy. Our discussion ranged on to the variety of stories attributed to the coastal Native culture. I said that not all the stories attributed to West Coast Natives were actually their inventions and told the group about my father's book, *Legends of the Evergreen Coast*, published in 1934. I can remember the hubbub during its launch, when I was a small child. Chief George Khatsahlano of the Burrard Indian Band was among the group of dignitaries in attendance. When he was asked his opinion of the stories, he just shrugged and chuckled. I am sure everyone thought my father had learned these stories from the local Native people. I do know that my mother did a lot of reading to help Dad gather material for his research, so she may have found the seeds that grew into the book while she was at the archives.

But just before his death I finally asked Dad about the authenticity of his writings, and his amused reply was that some stories are universal. Then I knew. The stories were his inventions. From all I have heard, he would likely not have been able to gather any from the local Native people—they had been laughed at and belittled for too long, so they were not about to expose their souls to any White person. As well, their stories were part of the warp and weft of their culture, woven into their existence on this earth, and they were hesitant to share them. (When my friend Lester Peterson was trying to learn the meanings of various pictographs in the Sechelt area, Chief Basil Joe's response was, "Hah, you White men stole our land, our forests and our salmon. Now you want to steal our stories." But Lester persevered, loaded up his fishing boat with a picnic and a case of beer, chose a lovely sunny day and took Joe cruising past the symbols about which his grandmother had told him when he was a boy. If Lester had not recorded those stories, they would have been lost with the passing of the old man. Lester included some of these stories in "Painted Rocks, Mystic Relics," an article published in *Pacific Yachting* magazine in June 1976.)

But all this was far from *Wood Duck* and Kano Inlet. On that stormy afternoon, I read my favourite *Son of Raven, Son of Deer* story to Paul by lamplight. "Ko-ishin-mit and Son of Eagle" describes the misadventures of Raven, who is a greedy fellow with a small beak and weak eyesight. He invites a large crowd of friends to dinner and promises his little wife that he will catch a salmon. His plan is to sit high in a tree over the river and dive down just as Eagle does when he goes fishing. Raven focuses on a disturbance in the river that grows larger and larger as he watches. When he dives down to grab what he thinks is a huge salmon, he bangs his nose on a rock that pokes up out of the stream as the tide recedes. Raven flops into the river and is rescued by Eagle, one of his invited guests. The results of Raven's attempt to copy someone else instead of using his own talents are no dinner, a swollen nose and damaged pride.

"That's a great story," said Paul, "but all that talk about feasts makes me hungry. Let's have a bite of our smoked salmon. Then we can go and see what this low tide has exposed."

The wind that tumbled the treetops and sent the eagles soaring in the updrafts did not reach us behind Cadman Island, so we rowed along in the shelter of a bluff and peered down into the clear water. Right under our noses were the spheres of huge red and purple sea urchins scouring the soft green algae from the rocks. I reached out with the long-handled fishing net and caught one. Its prickly spines waved frantically as I tried to untangle it from the mesh. Then we spotted our first abalone. Such excitement! Once our eyes adjusted to the refraction, we saw lots of them working along the perpendicular shore about three feet below water level. I put the urchin back in the water; visions of fried abalone far outshone the idea of raw urchin roe in sushi.

We had never harvested abalone before and had no idea how to go about catching these beasties. Like the little "Chinese hats" that cling to stones on the beach, these creatures use their suction cup foot to stay in place. I knew that once they felt threatened, they would grasp the rock so tightly I would have to break their shells in an effort to get them loose. Fortunately, we had the long-handled gaff hook and the fishing net in the boat. While Paul handled the oars and manoeuvred the boat closer to the shore, I hung out over the stern and gently lowered the hook and net into the water. A sharp lift under the edge of the shell pulled the unwary abalone loose, and a quick dip of the net caught it neatly as it tumbled down the slope. The undersized ones slipped right through the mesh, but the legal ones didn't escape. Unlike the huge abalone that used to populate Californian waters, the northern species is no bigger than a human fist, so we took six of them. Today you are not allowed to keep any of these delicacies because they have been overfished, but no such law was on the books in 1983. Oh, were we a happy pair! Supper was going to be a gustatory adventure.

That evening we experimented with ways of preparing these treasures. Surprisingly, slicing them thin and quickly flashing the slices through a hot frying pan in a dab of butter worked best for us. If these tidbits sat around on the plate and cooled, they became tough. I learned later that the traditional method was to give the morsel a swift whack with a hunk of two-by-four lumber to tenderize the muscle before cooking it. With homemade rye bread, a glass of wine, fresh abalone and a good companion, who could ask for anything more?

The sound of absolute silence woke us during the night. The trees no longer creaked and moaned, so we got up by five to begin our journey down Moresby's coastline. The strong winds may have gone, but they left behind some mighty lumps. Three swells in a row covered the length of a football field. On top of this heaving surface, a sharp chop developed from a southwest breeze that seemed to be freshening. This worried me because depth soundings were still scarce on our charts. Although the sails were moving us along briskly, they were also a hazard, partially obscuring my vision when I needed to be able to see where the swells were breaking over rocks.

As the morning wore on, the wind began to die. Our sails slatted back and forth rather than remaining full, so we doused the genoa, pulled the mainsail tight amidships to cut down on the roll and proceeded under power. The boat still tossed miserably in the leftover waves. Now we were getting hungry, so I went below to make a snack. It was uncomfortable down there and hard to keep my balance. When I set to work making hot chocolate, I got so nauseous bending over the stove that I decided to pour my cupful over the gunwale rather than lose it in a less dignified manner. It seems to me that mal de mer is partly fuelled by stress. I am usually at peace with the ocean, but the little trickle of fear that morning had been just enough to tip the balance. It was great to be up on top and not below decks. How could I not feel wonderful out here with endless ocean on one side and a gloriously unfamiliar stretch of shoreline on the other?

Later in the afternoon, off our starboard bow, we spotted what we thought was a fishing troller with a bright orange hull. If we held our course, we should pass close to it. I perked right up. Because of my brother's career in the industry, I was eager to see what a boat of that sort looked like when it was seriously at work. The trouble was, as we got closer it did not increase in size nor did it seem to be moving through the water. To add to our confusion, the orange colour was just too bright for it to be far away. We suddenly realized it was not a boat at all but a buoy of some sort. What was it doing out here so far from land? Had it come adrift from its moorings?

This apparition had a bright orange doughnut for a base on which was mounted a tripod crowned by a variety of equipment, including an anemometer, radar reflector and lights. There was a red- and yellow-striped panel fastened to the supports on one side. We could not see what was under the water, so we didn't get too close in case it was trailing lines that could foul our propeller. It appeared to be just moving with the current, so there must have been some sort of drogue to slow it down. On the base was painted a large "3" and on the striped panel

A bobbing buoy drifting off the unsounded, rugged west coast of Moresby Island was one of a group of buoys tracking the current flow along the outer coast of the island.

a large "2," plus a phone number but no area code. There was also a name that ended with "Geographic," but that was all we could make out from our cautious distance.

Paul decided to contact the Coast Guard to see if it knew who owned this lonesome baby. Sandspit answered our call. The officer was pleasant, and asked us to stand by while he made enquiries at Prince Rupert. We waited patiently, slopping around out there in the briny, but there was no farther contact. As it happened, our radio telephone had somehow switched to blinking double zeroes on the readout (probably my error; radio phones and I have never been on friendly terms), so we gave up and went on our way. We talked to the Coast Guard again later and learned that the buoy was one of a group tracking current flow along the outer coast, so it had not been lost at all.

The buoy was soon forgotten when the first albatross either of us had seen appeared over the grey undulation of swells. It floated on a cushion of air just above the surface of the water, peering right and left as it searched for food. A small flutter of its impossibly long, delicate wings, a slight dip of the head, and off it ghosted, savouring yet another morsel. The bird was so intent on the task at hand that it seemed not to have noticed us at all. Apparently these birds can stay aloft almost indefinitely, only coming ashore once every two years to breed and raise their single chick. To us, the albatross symbolized total freedom from the bonds of earth.

We were not totally free of those bonds. Yes, we were floating on top of a bed of water, but under our hull lurked the irregular tops of old mountains. The trouble was—where were they? The charts I had been able to buy from the government for this section of coastline assured me that the surveys had been done by a Mr. H.D. Pariseau in 1935–36 and that any parts of the coastline delineated by hairlines were compiled from aerial photographs only. As to soundings, they had been taken every 10 miles in a straight line about 10 miles out from the headlands. Every 30 miles the survey went offshore in a westerly direction for about 50 miles before heading southeast, following the coastline. It was obvious that we were on our own.

We stayed about a mile offshore, kept a regular lookout for any change in depth on the echo sounder and remained alert to surface disturbances that might indicate shallow water. Most harbours along the way were uncharted and appeared to offer little protection from southwest winds, although Security Cove, just off Inskip Channel in Englefield Bay, was almost oversounded. I got the sense that the frustrated survey crew had been holed up there during some ghastly weather and had kept from going nuts by measuring every square foot of the bay.

One of the things that most bothered me on the sketchy charts for this area was the lack of contour lines on the shore. In the days before Loran and GPS, these carefully researched landforms gave the navigator much confidence. Mountain ranges, sloping hills and sharp promontories were easy to identify. Without these guides, I had to count entranceways to inlets and try to peer down their lengths to decide just where I was. The entrance to Englefield

Bay stood out to some extent because of the cluster of islands that clogged the waterway. But even then, it was hard to separate islands from the background until we were close to them.

We had wanted to visit the abandoned Haida village of Kaisun, which was located just around the corner of the entryway to Englefield Bay. The problem was, none of the channels leading past that area had been sounded, whereas the central route was clearly charted, so I set our course down the middle of the passage that would take us to Security Cove, a good 10 miles from the open sea. As we entered the cove, I could not help feeling that security was all very well, but did it have to be so dull? We were surrounded by medium-sized second-growth trees that stood with their toes in the ocean. No great soaring mountains and no beautiful rock formations broke the monotony. It reminded me of Queens Cove on the west side of Vancouver Island. With all signs of earlier activity gone, there was nothing to distract the eye. But there was certainly shelter.

We caught a small salmon as we neared the entry to the cove. That solved the question of "What's for dinner?" and it also gave Paul bait for the crab trap. There were two streams that flowed down into the bay, each offering ideal crabbing conditions. So if the crabs liked our bait, we could hang around another day. It felt strange setting an anchor instead of tying to a mooring buoy, but we had a peaceful night even though a wind did get up after dark. There was no question about it: we were both strung out after the excitement of the past few days. Cruising these strange waters required a level of diligence far beyond that needed on the lower BC coast.

14 ENGLEFIELD BAY

Englefield Bay is one of the few meandering waterways that probe the outer coast of Moresby Island. Among other goodies, it contains an abandoned gold mine. It also offers miles of reasonably sheltered cruising. There are two well-sounded arms that lead off the main channel. On the charts we had, there were also great stretches where the only reference of depth ran right down the middle of the fairway. With no indication of landforms such as mountain ranges, we were on our own when it came to predicting wind direction. Some apparently sheltered bays turned out to be right in line with valleys, which encourage Venturi winds to hit down onto the water. In some places we went to bed with no idea of what horrors might develop should the weather change while we were sleeping. I am sure this is what Kathleen Dalzell was talking about when she cautioned about swinging at anchor behind Cadman Island. Wind that finds itself squeezed and redirected can become vicious.

We left Security Cove in the mid-afternoon for the short trip to Will's logging camp. Raindrops were coming down like hailstones, so we kept the awning up to shelter the helmsman. Of course, Paul insisted on putting out both fishing lines. It seemed as though we were continually dragging lines, but the speed at which we travelled was about right insofar as the little pink planing devices were concerned. As we rounded Percy Point, we went over a shallow spot and fish struck on both rods. This proved to be a challenge, what with an awning low over the deck and two rods to manage, but we landed both fish and got thoroughly wet in the process. At least we would not arrive at the camp empty-handed, although fish likely formed the major part of their diet already. Fresh fruit might have been more welcome.

Will had told us to expect a small camp, and that was what emerged through a veil of rain along the southwest side of Inskip Channel. Scattered along the shoreline were half a dozen little cabins, some for housing and some for storage and maintenance. All looked like they had been slapped together as the need arose. This was no major company listed on the New York Stock Exchange, but the setting was glorious: a shallow bay formed over the centuries by the outpourings of a steep stream, with the forest towering up into the mist, dwarfing the signs of man.

We eased in alongside the floating pen that kept the harvested timber from drifting off down the inlet. Unlike such enclosures farther south, this one was composed of large logs. Stepping out onto them to secure the boat seemed far less hazardous than climbing onto thin ones that tended to sink underfoot, but the splashing waves added lubrication here and there and tossed up treacherous ends of seaweed, so we both trod with care. The only sign of life on shore was a ribbon of smoke from the larger building, so we went back on board to dry out and have a bite to eat. We could visit in the evening when everyone would be relaxing in the cookhouse.

The walk to shore was an adventure in itself. Wavelets sloshing over the peeled logs created a distraction, but we both wore non-slip deck boots and managed not to slide into the saltchuck. It was high tide, and ghostly gleams of greenish white flickered underwater. I thought they were enormous shells of some sort, but we found out later that the crew ate a lot of deer meat and threw the heads out onto the beach for the crabs to clean off. I could have done without that grisly bit of information.

Everyone was in the cookhouse, the three-man crew and the young cook, and they made us welcome. The cook, Jacinthe Larose, an 18-year-old French Canadian girl, had made a dessert of Rice

Krispie cake topped with about half an inch of chocolate icing. Neither Paul nor I ate much sugar as a rule, so this hit us with a blast of energy that kept us lively well into the nighttime. This sugar high was accentuated by the caffeine of the strong coffee that came from a pot on the back of the huge cookstove. Jacinthe was the daughter of the prawn fisherman we met in Queen Charlotte City. He allowed the men to bunk on his boat any time they were in town.

When we asked how they could possibly run a logging camp with such a small crew, we learned that there had originally been four loggers, but one was in hospital in Victoria getting his bones mended and wired back together after a nasty accident. It was unlikely he would ever return to the trade. This had put a damper on their spirits, but they had other woes. The boss's wife was responsible for periodically towing the log booms through Skidegate Channel to Queen Charlotte City, a task that bespoke major skill at the helm. After traversing the Narrows, she would leave her tow at a booming ground shared by several small operators who hired a self-loading barge when there were enough logs to make a full load. Once her burden was safely penned up, she made the short run to Queen Charlotte City for supplies, fuel and parts before heading back to the west coast. On a trip three months earlier, she had radio-phoned when she was clearing the passageway by Chaatl Island on her trip back home. They waited and waited for her to arrive but never saw her again, nor was there ever any sign of her tug. A metal vessel swamped by a big wave would sink like an anvil.

We talked about the great challenge presented by Skidegate Narrows, and the boss, Leland Hakki, spoke of one of his experiences on that run. He said he could only take a short, small batch of logs through because of the awkward turns and shallow water. His tug needed five feet of water to clear the bottom, but at one point he had to go almost up onto the shore so he could swing the logs past a rock. When he had the tow far enough clear of the hazard, he put the helm hard over and gunned the motor so there was enough lean on the tug to keep the keel from touching bottom. On one occasion he did go hard aground. He said he should have known right away because the engine was going full bore but he was standing still. He saw the boom going by, so he unfastened the towline, let the logs go past and caught the tail end. The momentum pulled him free! This sounds so easy in print, but my mouth fell open with awe because I realized the enormous hazard the lone skipper faced in that situation.

Paul admires the butt of a huge log on the beach in front of the tiny logging camp in Englefield Bay. Logs were cut to about 10 feet in length for easier handling.

The camp had been quiet when we arrived because one of the tracks on the skidder was broken. The men had been struggling with it all day but lacked the necessary tool to fix it. When he heard what kind of machine they were using, Paul said he was familiar with it and promised to take a look in the morning because he likely had a few tools they didn't. We said our goodnights and made the precarious journey back to *Wood Duck*, which rocked gently in the swell with the rain and wind keeping the mosquitoes at bay. It was nice to know that our mooring was anchored to the carcass of an old donkey engine left over from a previous logging enterprise. There was no way we would drift off during the night.

Of course it was raining buckets in the morning, but we donned our gear and tramped off up the muddy trail to where the fellows were already struggling with their recalcitrant machine.

Paul was delighted to see that it was, indeed, the brand he knew from earlier years in California. The manufacturer, Food Machine Corporation of San Jose, had gone on from building food-processing units to producing all sorts of equipment needed by farms and industry in general. This one looked to me like a wartime tank with heavy metal tracks that were driven by smaller cogged wheels. It got into trouble when the operator was dragging a six-foot-diameter log down the muddy road and one side of the track slipped into a great hole. In the struggle to get it loose, a link in the chain snapped. The men had spent hours digging out under the track and isolating the problem. As it turned out, the tool kit lacked the half-inch wrench needed for the job. (It may have gone down with the tug.) But Paul had his, so he went back down to the boat to get it while I paid a visit to the young cook.

I asked Jacinthe how she managed the job, and she showed me some thin cookbooks by a famous French-Canadian chef, Madame Jehane Benoît, which were her mainstay. She added that the loggers had built a teepee in which deer meat could be smoked as one does a ham. Jacinthe told me the biggest problem was the lack of refrigeration at the camp. The propane fridge had packed it in, so she used ingenuity and a lot of canned milk. To keep things reasonably safe she had a screened cooler, but there was no ice. Since I had never once been too warm out there on the outer coast of the Charlottes, I could see where pioneer methods would work, but she certainly couldn't rely on old standbys like ice cream when it came to dessert. Nor in this perpendicular terrain could she keep a cow. Since the loss of the tug, they now had only a little aluminum skiff to get them to the trailhead that met a logging road with access to civilization.

That same aluminum skiff had Paul shaking his head when he came back along the floating pathway. The boat was half full of rainwater, so he stopped to bail it out and was shocked to find a beat-up, rusty .22 rifle skulking under the litter on the floor. When he asked the men about it, John Morris, the part-time halibut fisherman on the crew, chuckled and said it was his saltwater gun. When he hooked into a halibut that was a fair size, he had to put a bullet into its brain before he dragged it over the gunwale. Ability to aim was not a priority, but saving the boat from destruction by a flailing great fish was imperative. He reassured us that he cleaned and oiled the bore now and then so it wouldn't blow up in his face.

Paul was totally in his element amongst these fellows. Now that they had his half-inch socket wrench, they could get to work on the broken chain. As I approached, I could hear them grunting, muttering and laughing out loud every so often. The small crew likely enjoyed the distraction and help as well. It was clear that the best crew member on board any boat was a capable mechanic. Instead of being just another interruption, such a person's arrival at an outpost was a welcome event.

Paul told me that when they were finished, John was going to take him out to look for abalone and scallops for supper, so I might just as well put the two salmon we had caught into canning jars. The crew had had its fill of salmon and was looking forward to the results of John's dive. With that bit of information, I worked my way back down the hill, gathering scraps of wood as I went. Needless to say, they were sopping wet, but I could still use them once I had a good bed of coals in the stove. Hunching over the canner seemed to be my lot on *Wood Duck* journeys. Luckily, I found I could manage with a book in hand or a sketchpad on my lap.

In the early afternoon Keith Rowsell, a Fisheries officer, showed up on his large fishing boat with his wife and small son along for company. He moored near us and went off with the boss to inspect the area being logged. I felt relieved at his arrival, because I was concerned that the logs were coming down the hill close to what looked like a spawning stream. The richness of the soil attested to that fact. Spawned-out fish are often dragged 50 to 100 feet away from the water by scavengers, and their remains fertilize the soil. This makes for an extravagant growth of trees. The big spruce logs that floated in the pen represented centuries of good nutrition.

While the boss was off on the inspection tour, the other two crew members took Paul fishing. He was delighted to go along. He said that John had his diving gear and told them to just follow his bubbles while he searched for abalone and scallops. Each time he surfaced he tossed his catch into the skiff. He later told Paul that when he found a cluster of scallops, he counted off seven legal-sized ones before he took the next one. That harvesting method left an adequate number of adults to do whatever adults do. Then he rolled into the boat, and they went off to fish for halibut. He only kept those over 20 pounds. The smaller ones he eased back in the water, telling them to go away and grow up.

We were invited to dinner at the cookhouse that evening, and Jacinthe outdid herself. The food was superb. The fellows loaded up their plates and tucked in. I politely took a bit of everything offered with the intention of returning for seconds. No such luck. When all the plates were loaded up, the table was stripped of the first course, and I was left feeling foolish and a bit empty. So much for timidity around a logging camp table! I asked a logger about this later on, and he said that you could take as much as you thought you could eat, but woe betide anyone who left a scrap on the plate. What you took, you ate. There certainly weren't any scraps left on my plate.

Visiting that little logging camp in Englefield Bay was one of the high points of our trip. We thoroughly enjoyed meeting the crew, especially Will, who had taken us for the tour on Graham Island. To thank him, Paul decided to make a silver ring when we got back home. In his spare time he created lost wax jewellery, so he polished one of the agates we had gathered off the beach where Will went to recover from his breakdown. He made up a man's ring with the agate set in silver and mailed it to the address Will had supplied, but we never heard back from him. I can only think that the logging camp must have folded shortly after we left—the loss of the wife with the tug and the injury of one of the crew would have been hard to overcome—because Will was too polite a young man not to acknowledge such a gift.

15 EXPLORING THE OUTER COAST

We left the camp at six in the evening in a gentle wind that allowed us to sail right into Peel Inlet. This was one of the few areas that had been carefully sounded by the Hydrographic Service, so we felt confident moving along before the breeze. About six miles from the logging camp we found a sheltered spot in the lee of a small island, dropped the hook and rowed to the beach. I had used up so much firewood during the canning session on the boat that a trip ashore was crucial. Our only cooking device was the wood stove, and I had only wet wood left to burn in it, along with a small amount of pitch-laden pine that we had been eking out since the trip began.

After breakfast I mixed up a batch of bread dough before we began our exploration of the remaining three inlets in this system. Mudge Inlet was poorly charted and looked uninspiring, surrounded as it was by second-growth trees, so we just circled Colton Islet before heading back out around Recovery Point. There we disturbed a large colony of seals that were hauled out on the various rocky projections.

Paul was eager to explore Mitchell Inlet and the old gold mine just past Una Point. Our echo sounder was not encouraging when it came to anchoring, so I volunteered to cruise back and forth along the shoreline. I had the stove going and bread to bake anyway. Paul rowed to the beach and climbed up to the mine opening.

Except for bits of old, broken-down machinery, he found nothing to pique his interest and scrambled back down the hill.

Years later I asked my friend Joe Christensen about gold on the Charlottes. He was a prospector, and I knew that he had explored those islands. According to Joe, an old Native man at Queen Charlotte City claimed that before White people arrived, some of the Haida had used lumps of gold as anchors for their canoes because of the weight and malleability. The usual oval rocks used for anchors were chosen for the job because they were made from stone that was exceptionally heavy but was consequently hard to shape. The ones that I have hefted are formed of dark oval rock. They have a hollow pecked out around the waist to keep the retrieval line from slipping off. Sometimes this hollow is echoed by a second placed at right angles. The Haida found it was easier to carve a depression in the soft yellow metal, but when White people began to salivate over the shiny anchors, the more practical Natives hid them away from sight.

When mining began on the islands, the Haida realized that gold mattered to the White people, so they charged a high fee for any metal found. This infuriated the miners, who were not used to Natives acting in this manner. After the original flurry of activity, however, little gold has ever been recovered from the islands, and the moderate amount that was excavated went down on a ship.

The next inlet, Douglas, was also unsounded, although it did show the outline of the land. After hearing the Coast Guard warning that the southeaster was due to build to gale force, we had no other choice but to hunt for a safe anchorage there. We investigated a small bay beside Leslie Point that turned out to have a steeply sloping beach, but it would have to do. Our short anchor retrieval line was once again a problem, because it meant we had to anchor closer inshore than I would have preferred, but we made do with what we had. As it happened, during the early morning hours we woke to the gentle thudding of the cement keel hitting the ocean bottom. The boat had swung inshore of the anchor, but because we did not carry a kellet (a lead weight) that we could slide down the line to change the angle of pull and draw us into deeper

Paul found this abandoned heavy equipment at the gold mine near Una Point on Moresby Island. In spite of the occasional flurry of activity, little gold has ever been recovered from the Queen Charlottes.

water, we had to power up in the dark and move the boat. Aside from that we had a quiet night, confident that we had chosen a safe shelter after we were joined by a small salmon troller during the late evening.

We woke to find our harbour companion gone and with him most of the wind. A northwester was due that afternoon, so it seemed like a good time to head out and take advantage of the push it would provide on our way down the coast. As usual, the beleaguered Hydrographic Service had only managed to sound the centre of Moore Channel, so we kept to the middle of the passageway. Once we reached open water, our route down the coast was littered with hazards. It looked like someone had spilled a handful of seeds onto the chart. Depths and hazards appeared to have been thoroughly recorded, but one area that would have provided a nice passageway bore a note that assured me "the shoals immediately above (this point) not examined." That's enough to give any navigator the pip. Had it been a calm day I would have chanced it, but the farther we got outside the entrance the worse things began to look.

The choppy water and numerous uncharted hazards off Cape Henry drove us back to seek shelter and wait for smoother seas.

There was a huge tide draining the waterway behind us, and the southeast wind had just slowed down, not given up. The result of this collision of forces was a nasty chop that I found most distressing. The boat plunged up and down and rolled in every direction. I couldn't "read" the water, and there was no way that I could get us past these hazardous shoals in safety, so I said, "Paul, we have to go back. I don't like this situation at all." He swung the tiller over so we could beat a retreat.

On the chart I found a nearby bit of shelter in Hewlett Bay. It would do as a temporary anchorage until conditions improved. As we approached, we saw a fat doe on shore eating alder leaves, so we threaded our way quietly through streaming fronds of kelp. She totally ignored us. A low island stretched out its arms to each side of us, and its scraggly trees would help to screen most winds. Small islets within the bay partially broke up the swells, so we felt reasonably safe. It is always exciting to be able to anchor where you can see out into the ocean and observe passing traffic and impending changes in the weather.

Once everything was secure, we quietly got into the dinghy. The doe did not move until we were almost on the beach. Then she casually eased off into the forest. I clambered out onto the shore like the tin woodman. It was still raining and cold, so I had pulled the beavertail flap of my floater coat forward between my legs and fastened it to the hooks near my belly before struggling into layers of my old leaky yellow outerwear. This proved to be a most bulky arrangement. Paul laughed at the sight of me waddling like a fat duck as I moved among the slippery rocks. This didn't help me feel any better, but he certainly had a point. Even the gulls seemed to be chuckling. All the same, had there been a handy wad of mud, I'd have thrown it at him.

A stream that crossed the beach had been so badly eroded by the current rainstorm that a load of fresh gravel was spewed out over the shore and into the bay. This stream probably also provided the mud that gave our anchor a good grip. We strolled through the woods on ankle-deep moss, which told us that no loggers had ever worked this spot. Although the trees were weather-beaten and many years old, they carried no sign of man, nor were there any discarded bits of machinery. It didn't seem that fishermen spent much time here either, because the only litter on the beach was a plastic shampoo bottle stamped with Russian words. Luckily for our stove, we found knots on the outer beach. They would need to be scraped clean and dried on the outside but were welcome fuel nonetheless.

The southeast wind persisted into the afternoon, so we took a chance and stayed put. This would be a vulnerable spot if the wind changed direction, but neither of us wanted to backtrack. We had been delayed long enough. The boat kept up a restless roll for most of the night, because at high tide the ocean swells came over the rocks. I got little sleep and felt pretty fragile the next morning when we hoisted anchor at 7:30 and went out to have a look. If things were no better, we were prepared to return to Skidegate Channel and abort the whole caper down to Anthony Island, although Paul was most reluctant to quit. This time I set a course well into the middle of the channel and far out past any shoals. By nine o'clock the breeze switched around to the northwest, so we turned to port and set sail for points south. When there was no doubt we were clear of all obstruction, my confidence returned, so I left Paul at the helm and went below for a much-needed nap.

The mining company town at Tasu was our goal for the day, but we were certain there would be shelter at Kootenay Inlet along the way if we needed it. The tailwind held steady, so we sailed parallel to the coast, enjoying the return of the sunshine. It felt great to be back in the midst of our adventure. And wonder of wonders, the sun peeked through the clouds and glinted off the wavelets, spreading its rays down through the bottomless sea.

Just as I was passing cups of afternoon tea up from the galley, Paul shouted, "June, get up here. There's a freighter coming straight out of that mountain." Tea forgotten, I scrambled into the cockpit. We watched open-mouthed as an ore carrier that looked as long as two football fields came oozing out into the ocean like toothpaste squeezed from a tube. About three miles ahead of us was the narrow entrance to Tasu Inlet.

While we stood there, mouths gaping, a vessel larger than a seine boat shot past our bows. It must have been anchored in an indentation along the shore, and it roared straight offshore, then began dropping poles topped by black flags that fluttered and bobbed in its wake. We found out when we got into port that it was the fishing boat *Milbank Sound* out of Alaska. It was laying traps baited with squid to catch black cod. These traps went down 200 to 300 feet to lie on the ocean floor. A huge drum reeled out the line as the boat sped along.

My cousin Rod said that when he fished black cod years earlier, they used pre-baited hooks on a line that ran out of a huge coil at the same furious pace. Each coil was called a "skate" and carried 180 hooks spaced 18 feet apart. An eight-man crew handled more than 100 of these skates. They dropped an anchor with an attached flag, ran out five skates joined end to end, and then dropped another anchor and flag. He showed me the long scar on his thumb where one of the hooks had slashed his hand as it went snaking out of the coil and up over a gooseneck that carried it past the gunwale. It was a lucky thing that his flesh tore, because the line had an 800-pound breaking strength and could easily have hauled him over the side of the boat and taken him to the bottom, too. When I marvelled at the danger but also the effort that was required of the crew, he told me that they each got a share of the profits at the end of the season. With motivation like that, you certainly would not be a shirker, nor would your working buddies tolerate laziness.

I suspect that the cod in those days were considerably larger than those caught now. The ones we saw being unloaded from the

The mine site at Tasu, on the outer coast of Moresby Island, was in the process of shutting down when we were there. At its peak, the mine employed more than 170 men, but now it is deserted.

traps were no larger than a small salmon, whereas the chunks of smoked cod that my mother used to poach when I was a child in the 1930s came from a much larger fish with humongous bones. It was a treat we all looked forward to in the winter when she served the delicate flaky slices smothered in creamy parsley sauce. When I told Rod how much I had longed for the offer of a cod from the fishermen as we watched the fish being prepared for storage in the hold, he said that I would not have enjoyed it at all because it was only good after it was smoked. Otherwise it was too oily.

It was nearly 6:30 before we were snugly docked in the small-boat harbour in Tasu. We headed up the ramp for a quick exploration of the townsite. The first person we met along the way was Bill Ellis, the skipper of an old cruiser, *Single Jack* (Paul later told me the name referred to a special type of heavy hammer). Bill told us, "Hurry up. Dinner is served in the commissary from 5:30 to 6:30, and you might still have time to get something to eat." We thanked him and scampered off in the direction he had indicated. Sure enough, the kitchen was still open, but there was no one left at the tables. We grabbed trays, loaded our plates and gobbled down baked ham, sweet potato, pineapple and sour cream, some salad and ice cream followed by excellent coffee while the cleanup staff stood around and eyed us. This food was a real treat, so different from our usual bill of fare, but it left us belching from the air we had swallowed in our haste.

A quick inspection after dinner revealed a laundromat, so I got busy washing our clothes and Paul returned to the dock to visit Bill Ellis. I didn't find out until later that Bill was the publisher of the Dalzell books that gave us such great information about these fabled isles. He and his wife lived near Queen Charlotte City, so they were at home in these waters and had put many miles under the keel of their old cruiser.

While the washing machine was doing its work, I got talking to one of the residents who was busy with the same chore. He told me that the whole town was shutting down and would be empty within two months. At its peak of operations, more than 170 men worked the site. To accommodate the men and their families there was a swimming pool, gymnasium, workshops for recreational use, pubs, a hotel, a co-op store, a school and a small hospital. The housing consisted of apartments, dormitories and about a dozen single dwellings. He said that right now you could hardly move through the streets because of the crush of moving vans parked every which way. It was another North American ghost town in the making, right under our noses.

In their perennial search for copper, which served as their most precious metal, the Haida had discovered signs of it imbedded in rocks with other unusual properties. It turned out that what they had found was a mix of iron magnetite, copper, silver and some gold. In 1908 Henry Moodie and his father, two Haida who lived at Skidegate, prospected this area thoroughly. They guided the subsequent developer, but also staked some claims of their own. It became known as the Tassoo site and was mined actively between 1913 and 1917. No one paid taxes after that, so much of the land reverted to the crown. However, various companies owned the core area, and Falconbridge eventually came out on top. By 1967 this operation was crushing 7,257 tons of ore per day. Then came the usual cyclical drop in the price of copper, and the mill was no longer financially attractive. The ore carrier we saw coming out of that narrow slit in the mountains was likely the last one to leave.

I woke next morning with a distressed tummy. The unusually rich meal in the commissary had sabotaged my digestion. With a strong southeaster in the forecast, it was not hard to convince Paul to take the day off. We decided to explore some of the fingers that make up Tasu Sound. Those heaving Pacific swells could wait for another day.

If Tasu Sound were closer to a big city, it would be clogged with vessels of all sizes and shapes. It is a boater's dream: sheltered waters, pleasant views in all directions, nooks to tuck into at night with a stern-line to shore, lots of salmon and prawns. What more could a skipper ask? Since it was so isolated, we had it all to ourselves. Perhaps today there is a lodge and small runabouts or kayaks to rent, but in 1983 there was only the rapidly emptying town of Tasu. During its heyday, this charming area was probably well used on evenings and weekends, especially during the summer months, by mine families out fishing or water-skiing. Or maybe I was viewing it through rose-coloured glasses because it was a respite from slogging our way downcoast. Of course, we caught a salmon the minute we put our line in the water, but I drew the line at one. That was all we needed to fill the larder, and I was not in any shape to attend to a pressure cooker with its accompanying smelly steam.

John Morris of Englefield Bay had recommended Sunday Inlet as our next stop, so we headed out into the dying southeaster next morning. It was a long day of beating to weather, but as the afternoon wore on, the winds gradually died down to the point that we did better with the little Kermath putting along and the mainsail snugged firmly amidships to quiet the roll. Our little sabot trailed behind us like a pup on a leash. When we were heading into the wind it was no problem, but we had found during this journey amid Pacific swells that a following breeze was bad news. It often created a puff of wind that caused the little boat to scoot forward as it crested a swell, almost passing us to starboard as it slithered down the slope. A small inflatable tied down on the foredeck would have been safer, but we were stuck with what we had. Without it we would soon run out of fuel for our wood stove, which would be devastating but also boring, because we were both addicted to going ashore to explore beaches.

Just such a beach came into view along the way. It was Kwoon Cove, slightly beyond the entrance to Sunday Inlet, where we meant to anchor for the night. The large swells from the south passed right by, and any waves that remained revealed no rock outcroppings near the sandy shore, so we crept in past kelp beds. We were delighted to see an otter amidst the tangle, sleeping on his back with a frond wrapped over his tummy to keep him from drifting away.

Since this was our first outer beach on Moresby Island, we set off to examine it. My memories are of tangled, knotted seaweed, tufts of sage green coarse grass, a scattering of pieces of wood and a few old logs buried almost beneath the sand. To our chagrin we found day-old footprints, so we knew the flotsam had been well picked over. But we did gather four shopping bags of sun-dried knots for our hungry stove, and we certainly enjoyed sitting in the warm sunshine after all the drenching of the previous few days. On our way back down toward the water's edge, I spotted a small glass ball nestled among the debris in the morning tide line. Of course I picked it up, but I was sorry that Paul hadn't seen it first. He had yet to experience the thrill of discovery. Some people can walk right over things and not see them, while others, like my old pal Nellie Jeffery, never miss a thing.

We motor-sailed our way into Sunday Inlet and anchored near its head. Even there the breeze was still evident but did not seem to pose a threat. According to the chart, which had ample lines of elevation, there were no deep convolutions in the bluffs that surrounded the harbour, so it was unlikely we would be endangered by strong gusts during the night. It seemed incongruous that in this area the landforms were so carefully marked while the soundings in the ocean were few and far between, but the fact that this anchorage had been recommended gave us confidence. After supper all became quiet, so we went to bed cheered by the thought of making distance the next day.

16 ONWARD TO ANTHONY

My journal for August 7 begins *Great day! We awoke to dew and a light fog but no wind at all*. Long Pacific swells greeted our boat as we reached open water. These waves were huge and smooth, coming at us from the northwest for a change. The only chart soundings were in a line about two miles offshore, so we followed them, checking the depths now and then and keeping a good lookout. The engine ticked away for about four hours, but as the day wore on and a gentle northwest wind came up, we were able to throttle back and get some pull from the genoa. During the afternoon we passed another red doughnut buoy bristling with electronic gear. We were able to read the label, which said *Ocean Science Canada Current Survey*, so now we knew. This was number one. We figured there must be a number two bobbing around somewhere, because our first sighting had been number three.

By late afternoon we finally reached our last anchorage before Anthony Island. It was named, rather incongruously, Flamingo Inlet. No stilt-legged pink birds in sight, but there had been a Canadian Fishing Company steam trawler that inspired the cartographers when it came to providing a name for this long inlet. A small, shallow pocket off to the east side offered protection behind an islet, so we crept into Sperm Bay for the night.

According to Kathleen Dalzell, this inviting nook had been used by whaling skippers, who recommended Sperm Bay as a good place for small boats to anchor. It certainly looked good to us. We set the hook and heaved sighs of relief. Years later I read in William Hagelund's fine book *Whalers No More* that Sperm Bay was just about the only safe place at the lower tip of the Charlottes where boats could run for shelter during violent storms. In fact, the only truly safe spot was behind the same little island where we anchored.

The tide was low in the morning, so we delayed our departure while we went looking for abalone below the waterline on the dripping rocky bluffs. They were there, especially in the shadows. Their mottled, oval shells were so thoroughly disguised by the various bits of sea moss and weeds that had adhered to them that we had to look carefully to spot them. This species has survived by producing a rough outer shell to which hitchhikers can cling, cleverly hiding the shining mother-of-pearl that distinguishes the inside, so the abalone looks to be just part of its surroundings. Humans are not the only predators who savour them: land otter, gulls and mink, among others, are always on the lookout. Sunlight gleams off upturned discarded shells that litter the moss on just about every islet on this coast.

Most of the abalone were just below the surface of the water, so we employed the hunting technique we had used on Graham Island. I scrunched down on the floor of the dinghy, head over the transom, bottom up. Paul moved the little craft into position and tried to hold it steady while I did the gaffing. He had the toughest part of the job, but with a bit of patience and a generous lashing of humour we found enough to make two fabulous meals. All you eat of this creature is the large muscle or foot that it uses to cling to the rocks while it nibbles at its food. I slipped a knife between the opalescent shell and this white meat, scrubbed away the purple stain that disguises the outside and dropped each morsel into a container before returning the shell to the ocean. Other small creatures would feast on the remains. After storing the catch and slurping a quick mug of coffee, we upped anchor and turned the bow toward Anthony Island.

Our only chart for the area around the island had a scale in which a nautical mile measured about half an inch. Given the scarcity of soundings, I was unwilling to try the shortcut through the reef northwest of the island, although it looked navigable. We opted for safety over speed. One becomes a tad cautious when the keel of the boat stretches almost six feet down into the briny.

The terrain beside us was changing. As we travelled along the Moresby coastline we saw fewer mountain peaks. Landslides and sharp inclines were no longer in evidence. Instead of looking like the tree-clad gorges in China, where the skyline changes direction abruptly, all was tapering down to low hills clothed in scraggy trees. It was almost as though the island was giving up on the effort to exist and subsiding into the ocean.

But what an ocean it was! The shining swells dropped us down until the treetops disappeared from view and then lifted us up to reveal glimpses of the far-off curved horizon. It was as though we were on a child's slow-motion swing that offered tantalizing glimpses into distant fields when we reached the apex before once again descending toward the ground. The seas seemed to go on forever.

We were fast approaching the ancestral home of the Red Cod People. The Haida had been particularly fond of these large cod with brilliant orange-red skin that lived deep below the surface in places where the current swirled above them. When the cod was hauled up on a line away from the great water pressure of its familiar home, the air sac popped out of its mouth like an extra tongue. With bulging eyes and protruding sac, it looked startled by the whole business, as well it should be.

Much as we wanted to catch one of these delicious creatures, we could not do so in the breeze that pushed us toward our goal. I set a course well clear of the tip of Anthony to avoid the scattering of rocks and islets that lurk off the point. We changed our heading when the marker on Flatrock Islet came into view. This rock indicates the opening to Houston Stewart Channel, which separates Moresby and Kunghit islands. An adventure like ours would be a cinch nowadays with the aid of satellite navigation and echo sounders that read the ocean floor in front of your boat, but we managed in our humble way.

There was not a canoe in sight when we sailed down the outer coast of Anthony Island. How different it would have been when

Captain Robert Gray came in 1789. The people of the island had been awaiting his arrival ever since Captain George Dixon traded for sea otter pelts with Haida somewhere in the vicinity of Cumshewa Inlet two years earlier. If their neighbours farther up the coast had acquired new treasures by simply handing over furs, you can bet that the hunters around Anthony Island had amassed a goodly collection of skins and had been watching the horizon, ready to greet the traders and get down to some eager bargaining. The Haida were already astute traders, having dealt with mainland tribes for years.

They were also from a culture where important people demonstrated their superiority by the giving of gifts. In the Natives' view, these traders with their huge, well-equipped boats were obviously important people and would therefore be generous with presents. Gray noticed that they were helping themselves to the odd item, but he kept his mind on the job at hand. He wanted those furs to take to China, where he and the crew would earn a fortune. Gray probably never once thought that these so-called primitive people had their own culture or that they expected to be treated any differently than was the custom in the civilization in which he had grown up.

Where Gray succeeded, the next trader failed miserably. Captain John Kendrick, the senior officer on this first visit to Anthony Island, took over Gray's ship for the next trading session. He had a short fuse and was in beyond his mental and emotional depth. When he saw the chief, Koyah, and his companions helping themselves to things they fancied, he assumed that they were common thieves and he reacted violently, punishing them as he would have treated any crew member who disobeyed him. He chopped off Koyah's hair, slapped paint on his face and jammed his legs into the mouth of a cannon with the threat that he would blow him to kingdom come unless his people behaved differently. This massive disrespect and denigration of their chief alienated the Haida and turned Koyah into a fierce enemy. He had lost face and thereafter lost his position as the invincible leader of the local Raven Crest villages. His anger and subsequent treatment of

White traders polluted all future interaction between Whites and Natives on these islands.

When we finally arrived at the anchorage near the village, we were not greeted by flotillas of canoes, but we were greeted nevertheless. As we stepped out of our dinghy onto the beach, a long, lanky Native fellow unfolded himself from a hammock that he had strung between two trees. He welcomed us to the site, asked to see our permits, and then instructed us about how we were to behave at this historical place. We were to step carefully over any lumps under the moss and to leave everything as we found it. We could take pictures but not do rubbings. We thanked him and moved along the path with smiling faces and eager anticipation.

We knew that we would not be alone. For one thing, another sailboat was in the tiny anchorage with us. Also, we could hear voices. This was the first time in our travels since the gun-toting granny at Mamalilaculla that we met anyone else at these precious sites. As we came out from under the trees, we saw equipment on our left set up by archaeologists who appeared to be there for a long stay. Right next to this stood the remnant of a longhouse.

What struck me right away was the difference between the structure of this building and others that I had seen on the mid and lower BC coast. At Mamalilaculla there were two huge round posts at each end of the building, with curved hollows on top to support an equally large crosspiece. These supports were at the quarter and three-quarter spots at either end of the house. On top of this "arch" rested beautifully fluted logs that ran the length of the building to give middle support for the long roofing shakes. Large corner posts each held up logs that gave form to the eaves. Emily Carr's painting of the house at Chaatl Island shows a similar gable, with broad fascia boards going up to the peak, forming a closed end.

At the southern tip of the Charlottes, including Anthony Island, later builders used a new method to support the roof. The rectangular corner uprights had keyholes into which were inserted notched rafters that supported a number of longitudinal roof timbers. These long purlins were fairly thin as well. The liberal use of squared-off logs seemed to be unique to this particular kind of longhouse. It would have required a sharp metal shipwright's adze to form these timbers.

I was intrigued to see that the arrival of metal tools had encouraged these capable people to change their concept of how a dwelling could be made. It must have been something like the move to reinforced concrete from the old wood, brick and wattle structures that had dominated European construction for years. By making this change, the Haida were able to use lighter pieces of wood with shorter roof shakes and could build even larger longhouses in order to accommodate all the guests for a potlatch. The change in construction did not, however, change the underlying philosophy of the building. The house elements were named for the parts of the human body. The front support posts were the arms, the hind ones the legs and the longitudinal ones the spine. It was thought of as the container of souls. And so it was.

This may be why visitors who pause to listen can hear the soft voices and feel the presence of those who lived here. No White folk stayed on the island to dilute the intensity of the spirit world with Christian beliefs. In so many of our visits to abandoned Native villages, it seemed that White people's buildings had crowded out the old structures. Along with decrepit houses, there was usually trash, broken china pieces, parts of fishing boats and rusted bits of machinery littering the site, but here there was just the old cedar posts supporting an overgrowth of lichen and moss, with baby trees sprouting from the cracks. Aside from the archaeologist's equipment, there was no sign of White people's debris. At one time there were two other villages in sheltered coves on this small island where food from the sea was plentiful. Winter get-togethers were crowded affairs with plenty of food to eat, gifts to give and rich, symbol-laden ceremonies to keep memories alive.

When you entered a longhouse, you found yourself on the upper platform. Steps or ladders descended, sometimes through seven or more levels, until you were down in the area of the firepit. Florence Edenshaw Davidson told her biographer, Margaret

Blackman, that her ancestor Albert Edenshaw built a longhouse with 10 levels. Such deep excavations were only done in the most important houses, which would hold large gatherings. Each level below the top held intricately carved storage boxes, regalia or equipment. The top floor, where the heat from the fire collected, was the living and sleeping space. Smoke was guided out through the roof by a tilting vent that could be manipulated according to wind direction. Extended families shared the dwelling, with the chief's quarters usually at the far end.

There was plenty of room inside the chief's longhouse for the frequent parties where gifts were given away and oral history was presented to all gathered within. There were strict rules for the prolonged feasts that were an important part of these occasions. Those dining must take small mouthfuls, not talk during the meal, not discuss how good things tasted and not smack their lips. I learned these rules in 1985, when I arrived late at a banquet and gobbled down my food while visiting with a friend who sat across the table from me. A high-ranking Nisga'a man sat beside her, and I could see that he was experiencing some sort of stress. It was not until later that my friend told me that a Native person would have viewed my manners as atrocious. She explained that the reason for taking small bites and not talking while you ate was that this sort of behaviour could lead to choking, which would distress those around you. Had we been dining in a longhouse, there would have been no chatter during the meal. At intervals, slaves would have brought water and soft cedar-bark "towels" for cleaning grease off our hands.

Feasts were a time to impress guests. In *Cedar*, Hilary Stewart explained that "family status and wealth was reflected through the splendour of the great feast dishes, the elegance of the individual bowls and the complex intricacies of goat and sheep horn spoons." Self-respect was the watchword to guide behaviour, and the giving of gifts helped the hosts maintain their position in society. Adults' continuous effort to establish and maintain status they could hand down to their children created an industrious people. Hospitality and generosity came naturally to them. What a pity some of the early fur traders misunderstood this behaviour when it came to the distribution of gifts!

Judging by the number of longhouses shown in early photographs, there must have been a population of over 300 people on Anthony Island before smallpox arrived. This scourge killed so many that within 20 years of its appearance, only about 30 people remained, and the culture lay in shreds. The survivors left for Skidegate with Chief Ninstints in the late 1880s. But while they were here, it was a vibrant village filled with a close-knit group of people. Early explorers reported them to be well-muscled, especially in the upper body. The women were said to have rosy cheeks and lighter skin than those on the mainland. In fact, they made a cream to protect themselves from sunburn on long ocean voyages. According to Charles Lillard's history *Ghostland People*, this preparation contained grease and a powdered tree fungus that had been charred over a fire and ground into a fine black powder.

Unlike the mainland tribes, they appear to have left no family portraits. Emily Carr reported that when she visited the Nisga'a village north of Greenville on the mainland, she noticed that the human face depicted on a short totem could easily be a portrait of any one of the women who occupied the nearby longhouse. The eight-foot-high mortuary pole that I saw at Mamalilaculla in Knight Inlet was topped by the face of a man with his strong character shining through for everyone to see. I could swear he was just about to speak to me. Since he was not smiling and I was an intruder, I am not sure whether he would have welcomed me or admonished me for contributing to the demise of his people.

I saw no human faces on the remaining totem poles at Anthony Island, but the family crests displayed there were obviously of great importance to those who had commissioned the poles. These same crests were tattooed right onto shins, outer arms, chests and the top of the hands with great ceremony and feasting. Marriage within the crest was forbidden. The weather-beaten totems and the remains of burial poles were all that was left to tell the story of this powerful village with its strict laws and protocols.

As I turned to gaze out over the nearby beach, I spotted the old canoe skidways that speak of a maritime population. These narrow passages, cleared of rocks, would have been laced with peeled cedar poles held in place by small boulders to ease the chore of sliding the heavy dugout canoes up out of the water. These handsomely crafted hulls had been hauled out of the water stern first, so the knife-edged bow would not be damaged. An added benefit to this practice was easier launching in any sort of a wave conditions. The resting canoes were carefully shrouded in woven cedar mats to protect the wood from drying out and splitting lengthwise. I can

Most of the totem poles on Anthony Island were hauled away to museums, but many of those that are left display family crests, which were of great importance to the people who commissioned the poles. These same crests were tattooed onto shins, outer arms, chests and the top of the hands with great ceremony and feasting.

imagine slaves carrying waterproof baskets of seawater to dampen these "tarpaulins" in hot weather. The little cove where we stood was well protected by a small islet and must have been the envy of other villages where no such shelter existed.

Boats of various sizes were needed for going on seasonal harvesting trips and for everyday fishing and crabbing outings. In early summer when the halibut came close inshore to spawn, the men used ingeniously shaped hooks in order to catch these enormous flatfish that had such peculiar small mouths. The hooks were beautifully made and depicted various creatures. Hilary Stewart, in her book *Indian Fishing*, demonstrated several variations. If the hook was made of buoyant material, it was weighted; if it was already heavy, a carved wooden float supported it so that the fish could approach it when it stood upright. Fish sucked in the baited hook, but when they tried to forcefully expel it, the barb caught in the edge of their open mouths. As they carefully hauled away on the line made from the inner bark of the cedar tree, the fishermen thanked "the old woman of the sea" for letting herself be caught. When the fish were unloaded onto the beach, women skilfully cut the white flesh into thin slices and hung it on racks to dry for winter use.

During the late summer and well into the winter, dog salmon thronged into the short steep streams that tumbled down from the local mountains. Each family had its traditional harvesting place, with permanent fish-drying racks and also poles left in place to provide support for temporary shelters of split planks or cedar bark sheets. According to Hilary Stewart, there were many ways to catch these slippery fish, which have so much protective slime on the outer surface of the skin that it is almost impossible to maintain a grip. This protective slime not only helped the salmon slide past rocks on their way upstream, but also prevented casual capture by two-legged predators.

The fish were usually caught in traps or weirs, as it was much easier to lift the salmon from a trap, where you could slip your fingers behind the gill coverings. The Natives cut a slit down either side of the backbone, which they removed. Smoking preserved this part too, so that not a bit of meat was wasted. Fillets were not separated into halves as is done in our butcher shops nowadays. Instead, they were laid out whole over racks to air dry before being smoked over a slow fire. The meat had to be bone dry so it could be stored in carved cedar chests and remain safe to eat, unlike the juicy product we savour today with the advantage of refrigeration.

Haida caught crabs in traps that looked much like the flying-saucer variety in use today. They were made of netting woven with the strong spruce root fibre that was also the material of choice for making snares, beautifully decorated waterproof baskets and the hats that helped protect women's complexions from the sun.

Fish oil was another important part of the Native diet, but unlike the mainland, the Charlottes lacked the large rivers where eulachon returned to spawn. These little "candlefish" were a major source of oil for all the coastal people, providing not only nourishment, but also income for those who were in a position to reap this seasonal bonanza. The Haida made the hazardous crossing of Hecate Strait to barter for it, but they also found other local sources. They caught and boiled black cod and pollock (whiting), skimming off the oil that floated to the surface of the water and storing it for winter use.

Florence Edenshaw Davidson described how women and children went out in the fall to harvest the wild crabapples that grew in the valleys and near the beach. Before the arrival of large metal pots, they steamed this fruit in pit ovens until it was soft, then packed it away with seal oil in snug wooden boxes. Red huckleberries were cooked with salmon eggs, boiled until dry and were also stored in boxes, covered with a clean cloth (after fabric such as this became available). Florence's mother put roasted thimbleberry leaves topped with skunk cabbage leaves above the berry mixture, and the lot was covered in clean sand to force out any air. When the lid was tied on securely, the container was stored in the shade behind the house where it was cool. Salal berries were handled the same way.

The old cookbook that I inherited from my grandmother tells Victorian housewives to pack cooked fruit in clean bottles stoppered with a waxed plug and bury them under the earth in a shady place. Except for the lack of glass containers, the Haida women on the other side of the ocean had discovered much the same solution for preserving food.

In the early summer, when the sap was running, the women harvested the thin white cambium layer of the hemlock tree. This was steamed in a pit oven, pounded to tenderize, dried and stored away in small wooden boxes until it was needed. The resulting "cakes" were about half an inch thick and consisted of a pulpy fibre that was softened by moistening. This sweet delicacy was much prized as a treat. Alexander Mackenzie sampled some in

1793 when he was just upriver from what is now Bella Coola. He reported that it "resembled the inner rind of the cocoa-nut, but of a lighter colour." It was soaked, shredded and then dipped in fish oil. The Haida diet was rounded out with roots, berries, fruit, various plants and dried seaweed.

Life in the village was not all food gathering and work, especially for the men, who devoted many hours to gambling. Their game, which was somewhat like odd and even, involved short polished sticks of yew wood. One stick was coloured differently. The player divided his bundle into two lots out of sight of his opponent. These smaller bundles were wrapped in cedar cloth and passed rapidly from hand to hand under a cover. The opponent tried to guess which bundle held the coloured stick. This contest went on for hours. Luckily for the families, the gamblers could not wager the family rights to salmon streams, seaweed-gathering beaches, stands of cedar or other valuable resources.

In dry weather the gamblers usually sat outside on a wooden deck in front of the houses, watched avidly by the creatures of the family crests peering down at them from tall totem poles and by the figures on shorter mortuary poles, which contained the bones of their important ancestors. These short poles were carved so that the thicker part was uppermost, leaving room for the burial box. If someone died away from the village, he or she was cremated, and the bones were gathered and returned home to prevent enemy shamans using them for mischief.

Everyone seems to have worn body ornamentation of some sort. Noble women wore a lip ornament called a labret, which consisted of a carved oval disc inserted into the lower lip. The piercing for this appliance was done when a baby girl was just four days old. During this ceremony she was held by her father's sister, who celebrated the occasion by giving a feast. At first only a small ivory plug was inserted; over the years, new plugs were inserted with gradually increasing diameters until the labret was several inches across. Both boys and girls had their noses and ears pierced. There could be up to five holes in each ear, with little carved ornaments of seashell held in place by small plates of copper.

One of the many common crest figures depicted on totem poles is Frog. In many coastal First Nations, Frog indicated spring and new life.

Girl babies were valued because they brought wealth to the family in the form of a husband who moved into his wife's childhood home for a period of time and laboured for her father's benefit. Women were also expected to produce many children. According to Florence Edenshaw Davidson, bearing 10 children was the norm and was accomplished with minimal fuss. To avoid soiling the longhouse, the actual birth took place in a separate shelter. The afterbirth and bedding were burned, and the woman went into seclusion for 10 days. The name given to a baby was governed by the Haida belief in reincarnation and was celebrated with a small potlatch.

At the time of her first menstrual period, a young girl went into isolation in a separate shelter for a number of days. Only women could visit her, and her father's sister instructed her on proper behaviour as a wife. An arranged marriage was performed shortly after her "coming out party," which consisted of a large potlatch given by her father.

Because of strict taboos, menstruating women retired to a separate shelter while the grandmothers and youngsters did the chores. When a group of women lives in the same dwelling under natural light, their cycles often come to follow a common rhythm. To serve the need for absorbent material, the Native women harvested the inner bark of young cedar trees over a two-week period in the spring. Hilary Stewart, in *Cedar*, reported that yellow cedar was preferred, if it was available, because after it was pounded it was softer and could be used for baby diapers and other absorbent needs.

Artwork was a male domain. Perhaps the women were too busy with the babies that came every few years and with all the basket making, food preservation and cooking. Even into the 20th century, women such as Florence Davidson had her husband design the figures that she sewed onto her button blankets, although on one occasion she got up very early in the mornings so no one would see her painting the design on a large canoe that her husband had built. This was more a matter of protocol than a reflection on female creative ability, as artistic talent is not gender specific.

The houses that gave these men and women shelter on Anthony Island are now no more. A few grey poles and corner posts are all that remain. The people are dispersed, leaving only broken reminders of a vibrant population that once called this small island home. Yet the voices remain in the whispers among the trees and the sigh of the wavelets that ripple onto the beach where so many feet have trod. We filled our camera with pictures and turned to leave, taking with us only the wonder of the place.

17 ROSE HARBOUR
AND THE EAST COAST

According to the guidebooks available at the time, our anchorage at Ninstints was no place to be during big southeast storms. Since weather can change suddenly, and since we did not want to clutter up the tiny bay, we moved along into the gap between Kunghit and Moresby islands, to the shelter provided by Rose Harbour.

This charming name must have produced many a chuckle from the whaling fleet that arrived in this port with huge whale carcasses. The stench that resulted from rendering blubber into oil and cleaning the baleen plates used to stiffen ladies' corsets would permeate all surfaces. Huge bones, stripped of flesh, were stacked in great piles waiting to be ground into bone meal. The meat had to be cooked and then dried before it was ground up to make animal feed. The accompanying smell of death and decay would never be mistaken for attar of roses!

Commercial whaling didn't begin in BC until the early 1900s. Before then, American interests had established whale-processing plants in Alaska and Washington State that were producing good returns to justify the huge initial investment, but Canadian interests were still wrapped up in the lucrative seal hunt. In 1894 sealers harvested over 100,000 seal pelts, but the shrinking size of the herds and the increase in competition and international regulations began to turn their attention toward the whale hunt that was obviously happening in Canadian waters with no Canadian participation.

According to William Hagelund, whose book *Whalers No More* is an outstanding source of information on the BC whaling industry, Captain Sprott Balcom of the Victoria Sealing Company saw the possibilities offered by whaling. In 1904 he and Captain William Grant skilfully navigated government regulations and began building their first plants on the west coast of Vancouver Island. By 1907 they had built the much larger operation at Rose Harbour, near the home waters of the bulk of the whales. In the first six weeks of operation it processed 80 whales, and at the peak of activity there were up to 160 workers.

The plant consisted of about a dozen buildings of various sizes on pilings, plus the double slipway for hauling the carcasses into the work area. There was also a long dock to accommodate freight boats and to store the coal that fuelled both the power plant and the chaser boats. Small residential buildings were on shore. The workers reported the site was idyllic—aside from the smell.

The Japanese who made up the majority of the employees enjoyed the plentitude of sea life that supplied their tables with delicacies. Forget the meat and potatoes required by the White folk. Here was sushi heaven with abalone, crabs, scallops, fish of all kinds and seaweed to go with the rice. For a while these enterprising fellows even tried canning abalone for shipment to market. All that they lacked to make this pure heaven were their wives and children.

When the Japanese were interned and moved away from the coast during the Second World War, the factory lost its skilled employees. That blow, and the dwindling population of whales, hastened the death of this working port in the 1950s.

In 1983 we could see little of the old factory from where we were down on the boat. The three mooring buoys were occupied, so we had to drop the hook east of them. In a port where discarded machinery probably litters the floor of the bay, an anchor retrieval line is a good idea. We had no trouble, but that could have been dumb luck. I learned years later that we had chosen the spot where the long dock used to sit. I could not see if the remains of old piling stubs were still there, nor was I looking for them. As in most of these outports, most structures were built out over the water, so it's best to be cautious when dropping an anchor.

It was a rocky harbour, almost entirely landlocked, but beautiful, surrounded as it was by greenery. The incredibly clear, cold, swiftly moving water sparkled in the sunlight and was alive with colourful sea creatures. Morning brought a low tide, so we crossed over to the other side of the passageway and searched the bottom for a weed-free area where the anchor could get a grip. The rocky outcropping to the left glistened with a collar of golden bladder-wrack that spoke of hidden delicacies. But the first order of the day was firewood. We went to examine the beach to see what treasures it held.

Paul had yet to experience the joy of finding a glass float, so when I spotted a small one nestled among bits of debris, I left it where it was. He roamed all the way to the end of the beach but found nothing, so I called him back and said the spot where I was standing looked good. I pointed out pieces of old cork floats as well as some newer foam ones. He almost stepped on the ball before seeing it. He glanced at me, but I kept busy turning over other things and pretending not to have noticed.

"Did you know this was here?" he asked suspiciously.

"Oh my, no," I replied, lying innocently. "What did you find?" The reward of seeing the joy in his face when he showed me the treasure erased any feelings of guilt.

Another delight was the quantity of dry bark scattered along the high tide line. We had not seen a bounty like that since we hit the west coast of these wild islands. Before long our plastic shopping bags were bulging with precious fuel. We piled it in the dinghy and strolled over to examine the rocky point. Sure enough, abalone were everywhere. How could we resist this free meal? In fact, two or three meals.

Because we were on the beach before seven in the morning, there was lots of time left that day to mosey on toward Ikeda Bay. This inlet looked like a good place to find shelter for the night. Neither of us was sorry that we were finally back on the east coast of the Misty Isles. We had been lucky when we travelled on the empty outer side. The weather had been kind to us, and we'd managed to avoid trouble, even though the charts were almost empty of notations. We'd had adventures to last us many years and had seen the fabled old village on Anthony Island. Now the charts guiding us had all those useful little details that make cruisers feel secure. It was August 10, which left us three weeks to get back to the Lower Mainland and our teaching jobs, and we were prepared to briefly explore this area, stop in at the hot springs and then head back across Hecate Strait.

Ikeda Bay was one of the few places where we had a disagreement about where to anchor the boat. I favoured the left-hand shore, a little farther into the bay and under the shelter of a low bluff, but Paul insisted on anchoring in the shallows near a stream mouth. He owned the boat, so there could really be no argument. As it turned out, neither spot would have been secure. A wind began hitting the hull a little after midnight. I got up to have a look at the shoreline from under the edge of the back deck awning, but everything seemed to be normal. I asked Paul if I should let out a bit more line, but since I was unable to report anything amiss, he thought it would be all right as it was. Shadows of our earlier disagreement about where to anchor may have influenced that decision. I should have gone up the companionway and stood out on the back deck to check our position, but I did not do so. I did notice that the boat seemed to be yawing more than usual, which was likely what had wakened me in the first place. But it began to rain, so I snuggled back into bed.

About two o'clock a sharp rapping on the hull woke us abruptly. Then we heard a voice. Paul struggled out of bed and slid back the hatch. Sitting in his skiff in the pouring rain was Keith Rowsell, the Fisheries officer we had met at the logging camp. He was anchored just down the bay from us. "You're dragging anchor," he shouted. His wife had been up in the night to check on their son and noticed that our masthead light was much closer to them than it had been earlier.

Paul thanked him profusely, pulled on his rain gear and got the motor started. I bundled up and joined him on deck. While he hauled away on the line, I kept the boat moving ever so slowly forward. He set the anchor again, let out more line, sat up to watch for a while, and then crawled back into bed. To further compound our embarrassment, this all happened once more before first light. At that point Paul drew the anchor completely clear of the water to check the flukes for debris and then let out all the line in the storage locker. Our wandering boat did no more drifting during the black of night, but that was likely because the storm had passed. We woke to the noise of a giant sunfish leaping clear of the water, then splashing back down—a most unusual alarm clock.

Our first project that morning was to row over to the Fisheries boat and offer Keith our sincere apologies for getting him up and out into his skiff in the wind and rain. He chuckled and said that he had been anchored in the bay years ago on a big halibut boat. When a storm hit, they ended up with two anchors out and still had to run the motor all night to keep from being pushed into the strait. Certainly on the chart the bay looked innocuous enough, although the compass rose covered the area that would indicate gullies or breaks in the mountain range that could act as a wind funnel. The fishermen we talked to at Tasu had recommended Jedway Bay, just around the next point, as good shelter, but we wanted to explore the old copper mine that had made Ikeda Bay a busy and profitable place, so here we were.

We had little information on Arichika Ikeda, for whom the bay was named, when we were there. We did know that he had brought in a paddlewheeler that had served the gold rush in the Yukon. He had this roomy craft set up on supports on the shore to serve as a bunkhouse for his workers. The rainy Charlottes weather had made short work of that structure, nor was there much else on shore to tell the story of the venture. We read that Arichika, nicknamed Archie, had come here first as a fisherman and that his discovery of ore was accidental. The discovery may have been accidental, but the story of the man himself is anything but. He was a visionary who did nothing by halves.

In 1984, Gordon G. Nakayama wrote *Issei: Stories of Japanese Canadian Pioneers*, because he rightly felt that Japanese Canadian contributions to this country's prosperity had been sadly neglected in our history books. Among the stories he included was that of Arichika Ikeda, a well-educated fellow, born in Japan, who went to Tokyo as a 16-year-old to study English and read Chinese classical literature. Not your typical teenaged kid. From there he went to Nagano to train to be a doctor, but he found this was not his calling. He tried various ventures in Japan before heading to California. News of the gold strike in the Yukon brought him north with products for sale to the miners. He tried his hand at gold mining, but when he noticed the abundance of salmon available—and the waste of less popular species like chum—he hurried back to Japan to get financial backing for a plan to ship salted fish to Japanese markets.

By 1904 he was also shipping salted herring to China. Once this enterprise was well launched, he handed it over to another Japanese businessman and went looking for new fishing opportunities, using a good-sized schooner that he based in what later became Ikeda Bay. It was here that he noticed the large outcropping of copper ore. The Haida had mined copper on the east coast of Moresby Island for generations, but never on the scale dictated by Archie's entrepreneurial spirit. In 1906 he secured financing from Japan to build a railroad and wharf and to buy mining equipment so the work could begin. The Canadian government of the day was so pleased with this development that they named the bay after the man. A picture in Nakayama's book shows Ikeda standing with visiting dignitaries under an arch of cedar boughs during the official opening of the dock and facilities.

The mine went through extremely busy times and was mothballed during periods when the price of copper slumped, as it is prone to do. Archie built an attractive house for his wife and their son, Arimoto. I would guess that he also had a house in Vancouver, given his belief in the value of a good education. Izo Arima, who was a friend of Archie's and who spent four years at Ikeda Bay, wrote in his diary of Archie coming up from the city to get him started on a surveying and refurbishing project that took place while the mine was temporarily shut down.

But it was not all work and no play while Izo and Archie were together. They hunted waterfowl, fished and trapped octopi. Izo said that the octopus made a little cave in the sand under the edge of a big rock. He could spot the den by the broken crab shells that littered the small depression in front of the hideout. According to Izo, he just had to reach in with his hand, grasp the octopus between the top of its head and eyes, and pull it out of its nest. He said it was impossible to get it out by grasping a tentacle, but I would be afraid of sticking my finger in its beak.

The Japanese men trapped octopi in order to eat them. Izo said that with all the local delicacies available for them, they only needed to buy tea, rice, miso, soya sauce, sugar and salt, which came up from Vancouver by freighter along with the mail. He also noted that they got free whale meat from the Japanese workers at Rose Harbour.

Archie was curious about the surrounding territory, so when the weather was good they took a small open sailboat and went to scout the area around Burnaby Island, where the falling tide put them aground when they were trying to navigate the narrows. While they were on this trip, they ventured into a narrow bay on Moresby Island, built a small fire, cooked their supper and slept the night in the little boat. When the tide was low in the morning, Izo saw tall, thin, dark sticks planted upright in the mud across the mouth of the stream at the head of the bay. Archie told him that when the salmon runs arrived, the Haida would wait until high tide, pile branches across these sticks to form a porous dam and catch the fish that were now trapped by the temporary weir.

At the start of the Second World War, the price of copper rose, so the mine went back into full operation. Employees who had scattered throughout the province returned happily to work for this kind, generous man. One Sunday Archie felt like taking a break, so he and some of the men went to visit Hotspring Island, about 25 miles upcoast. As they approached, Izo noticed the verdancy of the local vegetation, which he assumed was the result of warmth coming from the earth. They climbed to the top of the hill and followed the hot springs down until they found a pool cool enough for a good soak. He said the water was so clear they could see their feet.

Archie built a small cabin there, ensconced a cook/caretaker, lined one of the pools with cedar planks and used the island as a spa for crew members who became ill. If this were true, it happened after Izo went back to the city, because he does not mention it in his diary.

Needless to say, we looked forward to visiting these wonderful springs after that horrible night of the dragging anchor. A long soak in hot mineral water would do nicely even without the kind ministrations of Archie's chef, and we left Ikeda Bay in eager anticipation. We were not disappointed.

As luck would have it, we arrived at Hotspring Island just as a huge American cruiser left. An old fishing boat was anchored nearby, and there were a few tents on the island, but that was all. These days it would be abuzz with activity. We stuffed our bathing needs into a couple of grocery bags and rowed ashore. Just as I was stepping out of the boat, a wave rocked the dinghy. I stumbled, and my towel and clean underwear spilled out into the saltchuck. Bother! I grabbed as much as I could before it sank, but was left with a boot full of water and badly damaged pride. Now I really needed the restorative power of the springs.

The bathhouse was a primitive cedar structure with windows to seaward. These openings faced the wind, but a cooling breeze was welcome to allay the heat generated by a grand flow of steaming mineral water. We found a pair of cast-iron enamelled tubs and two large black hoses carrying water, similar to the setup at Nascall Springs near Ocean Falls; unlike those at Nascall, one of the hoses was labelled *Hot* and the other was *Scalding*. We positioned the rubber dams over the drain holes, let the tubs fill to the overflow ports, disrobed and sank into total bliss with just our knees and noses out in the air. When our fingers and toes began to look like prunes and not a muscle was left in our bodies, we clambered out and dried off. Feeling like a sleepwalker, I struggled into my wet clothes. Ah well, what's a little dampness after all that bliss?

We motored over to a small cove on nearby Ramsay Island, where we found two other boats riding at anchor well into the bay. This proved to be a rolling roadstead for us. Because we were the late arrivals, our boat was sheltered from open water by only a reef and cluster of small islets, but it would have to do. We celebrated our eve of departure with a great feast. That morning we had caught a female coho salmon, so there was immature salmon caviar, poached lightly in lemon juice and water and then dipped in soya sauce; steamed saltwater snails in garlic butter; and a tart white wine. The main course was potatoes baked in foil in our little wood stove, a salad made with mixed sprouts and avocado (thanks, Tasu), and barbecued salmon cooked between the layers of a toaster rack over hot coals that had been scraped into one end of the firebox. Everything tasted divine, because we had much to celebrate and pure fresh food to make the occasion special. I don't think either of us would have traded this meal for one served in the fanciest restaurant in the world.

"You know, Paul," I said, as I reached for the teapot, "we didn't get to visit many old village sites after all, did we? And we've run out of time to explore this inner coastline, although I'm happy about what we were able to do. How do you feel about what we accomplished on this trip?"

"It's been one of the highlights of my life, June. But as to how I feel about the success of our venture, well, I'll be able to answer that question better when we are safely back on the mainland side of this waterway."

"With the good luck we've had so far, we'll be fine," I grinned as I filled his empty cup.

I learned years later that had we travelled a few miles farther up the eastern coastline of these Misty Isles, we would have begun to see the clear-cut logging that was destroying the wild beauty of Moresby and caused the uproar that eventually resulted in the creation of a national park. No more logging would lay waste the centuries-old majestic forest.

After supper, Paul rowed ashore to bury the food scraps while I cleaned up the galley. When I tried to fill the kettle to get it ready for the morning, nothing happened. The water tank was empty. Luckily we had two large thermoses full of drinking water and plenty of tinned juice on hand, but we would have to be thrifty until we could find a "sweet" water supply. Meanwhile, the mosquitoes were sneakily moving in for the night. With no wind, and the few boat openings draped in netting, the boat soon became miserably hot. We put in a restless night sweating and swatting. I could not hear the whine of these little beasties, but I could certainly feel the itch, so my memories of Hotspring Island are a combination of bliss and bites. However, the satisfaction of knowing that we had accomplished our goal would last for both of us.

18 NEXT STOP: CAAMAÑO SOUND

The next day we were headed toward what appeared to be an almost featureless coastline. To get there we had to cross one of the most treacherous waterways on the coast with a radio beacon, a wonky compass and an old-fashioned depth sounder as our only guides. My navigational skills were going to be put to the test.

The weather report on the morning of our departure sounded benign. No storms were forecast, so Paul fired up the trusty Kermath engine, we raised the mainsail, and Paul attended to the anchor while I nudged the boat gently forward into the early mists of dawn. And "gently" it was. With no fuel gauge, we decided to set the speed at about three and a half knots, thereby guaranteeing a slow, tedious crossing. Should the wind get up, we would certainly use it, but for now it was a case of settling down and motoring along through what turned out to be a pleasantly sunny day. By noon we were taking turns nude sunbathing on the front deck.

In the early afternoon a breeze riffled the water from the southeast. On went the clothes, out rolled the genoa and off went the motor. Oh the magic of it: no sound except the burble and hiss of water sliding past the hull; no exhaust fumes hiding the delicate aromas rising from the ocean, the exhalations of all the creatures of the sea; no need to speak louder than a low murmur; no worries about draining the fuel tank. As long as the wind remained moderate, we were in no danger. Our joyfully brisk sailing was short-lived, though. Within two hours we were almost becalmed.

The fickleness of the breeze is just one of the challenges of being a sailor, but we made do with what came our way.

The day wore on interminably, with just enough wind coming now and then to keep the knot meter wavering around three knots. Since we needed to conserve fuel and were facing a journey of 73 miles to get as far as the pass at Caamano Sound, it seemed a wise, though tedious, decision to give the motor as long a rest as possible. We took turns on watch because we knew there would be a long night ahead of us. A heading of approximately 53 degrees would take us to the pass, but current drift and breezes could skid us to one side or the other during the long crossing. A heading of 40 degrees would take us from Hotspring Island to just north of the pass, where a radio beacon sent out a continuous Morse signal to guide mariners across the sea. If we latched onto this radio beam, we could be sure of staying on track to our destination.

These beacons require good hearing on the part of the navigator, so Paul was stuck with that task. Once he picked up the signal, he moved the receiver back and forth until the sound reached its weakest point, the null. He then recorded the direction of this signal. The theory behind choosing the weakest position is that deciding the volume of the loudest noise is beyond most of us, but we can usually figure out when the sound vanishes. So it is easy to see that my deafness rendered me useless.

When I crawled into the bunk after dark, I knew there were still many miles to go on our journey across the strait. One challenge we faced was that the radio beacon was located about eight miles north of the light indicating the left-hand side of the pass to which we were heading, so if we just aimed for the signal, we would run right up on shore. I had worked over the chart during the day and determined that the light we needed to find was on tiny Jacinto Island. Beside the coloured symbol for the light was the note "Fl 4 sec 76 ft 5M," which meant it flashed every four seconds, was located 76 feet above water level and could be seen from a distance of five miles away. I figured that by the time we saw the light, we could alter course as needed and abandon the radio signal.

This all sounds very chancy and assumes no fog or low-lying cloud to interfere with our vision, but the weather report remained positive, so we hung in there. Ideally I should have located at least two radio beacons, recorded their compass direction from our craft, and marked on the chart where the signals met, but this sort of navigation was more than I was prepared to handle. By this stage of my boat-racing life, I had become dependent on the Loran to determine the position of my boat, the direction to be steered and the other navigational details that I needed to know. In a word, I had become lazy.

Fortunately for us, no storms or fog rolled in to complicate our adventure. I had already decided that if the weather deteriorated to a point where we were in real danger, we would run before it and head for Alaska. I don't know what we could have done in a raging northwest gale, other than toughing it out. There were too many rocks and hazards farther south along this part of the coast to take a casual approach unless one was already familiar with the area. Also, I was not entirely confident that the rigging could handle a major blow. But when a glimmer of light became visible on Jacinto Island, we knew where we were, could abandon the radio beacon, adjust our heading and relax a bit. Paul took his good hearing below for a well-earned rest, and I went on watch with my bum ears and keen eyesight. My nap had invigorated me, so I reached for the tiller with pleased anticipation. We were finally nearing our goal.

In the blackness of night, the sea had become almost glassy smooth and was barely disturbed by the lightest of breezes, which appeared to be aiming right for the coast. With this infinitesimal bit of a push on the sails, *Wood Duck* slipped gently along, zippering up the ocean's shiny coat in our wake. The new compass reading would take us just clear of the light, which showed itself more brightly with the passage of time. However, the current began pushing us steadily to the right. I knew this was happening because the compass bearing on the light revealed smaller and smaller numbers. Ness Rock lived down that way, so I had to keep adjusting our heading. When lights from anchored fishing boats began showing up from behind Jacinto Island, I had to overcorrect because it was obvious our vessel was still being swept to one side of the desired route.

It was four in the morning before we finally came within a mile of the light station. I was able to get a reading on both the radio signal and the light, which meant I could finally mark our location with some accuracy on the chart. From this point, if we could manage to stay on a course of 91 degrees, we would pass near the tip of Rennison Island and be able to pull into the anchorage that had been recommended to us by a kindly old Norwegian fisherman at Port Hardy. Another alternative was to seek shelter in Gillen Harbour, behind the Jacinto light, but it was still too dark for us to navigate through the passageway into an unfamiliar place, so we carried on with our original plan. In retrospect, given what happened next, it would have been better to lurk around the area until daybreak so that we could find our way into Gillen, but our judgement was clouded by exhaustion.

Dawn arrived, and our small boat was barely moving. By this time Paul was awake and reported that there was enough hot water left in the thermos for some instant coffee. I was just about to suggest that we start the motor when a breeze from the southeast began to tickle my cheek. "Hey, Paul, we're in luck. The boat's moving again, and if I pull in the sails a bit I think it will just nicely keep us going on this heading."

"Great news," he said. "Coffee coming up in a jiffy." He bundled himself up in his warm floater coat, and we sat together in the cockpit savouring the almost hot drink.

A dark streak of cloud up ahead should have alerted us to shorten sail, but I guess we were too happy and content to be nearing the end of our marathon trip to be thinking defensively. In no time at all, we were nearly knocked down by a blast of wind. We struggled to put one reef in the mainsail and furled some of the blessed genoa with the help of the winch. As the wind built up strength, it came more and more onto our nose. We were unable to hold our course, and headed off about 20 degrees. The trip we hoped would take three hours turned into nearly six as we were pushed farther and farther left of our goal. We were lucky this fierce wind had held off until we nearly reached shelter. Certainly Hecate was living up to its reputation, and it should have come as no surprise to us novices that a gale could build up in a matter of minutes.

The closer we got to Rennison Island, the more debris we met. The very high tides had lifted a great many logs off the beaches, and places like this, where the currents run in and out, tend to collect driftwood as it moves out to sea and then is swept back with the next change of the flow. The increasing daylight allowed us to spot the deadheads that lurked just below the surface, waiting to punch a hole in the hull or damage the rudder in passing. The fishing boats that had been anchored in various nearby bays were all out in the area off Oswald Point doing the reverse waltz, where each boat in turn gets to sweep past the shoreline and troll through the eddies where the herring hide out and the salmon are feeding. There is a strict protocol in effect as everyone gets an even chance at filling his lines with these shimmering beauties. Woe betide the ignorant person who tries to butt into the line. In a dangerous job where your life depends on getting help when emergencies arise, you take no chance of being ostracized.

These fellows were equally harassed by the accumulation of driftwood. We had to keep on the starboard tack much longer than we wanted to, because the wind was driving the trolling boats farther in behind Oswald Point, and the driftwood was sweeping in with the incoming currents. Finally we passed the end of their promenade and were able to fall onto a port tack and head for shelter. We were getting too near a rocky point and felt we'd be more manoeuvrable under power, so after reeling in the headsail, Paul went up on the top deck to haul down the main. I was steering with my knee and attending to the trailing edge of that slippery cloth when we were hit by a sudden blast of wind that blew away my favourite old blue toque. Luckily, it spared Paul. I muttered a few bad words as we bunched the flailing cloth and lashed it with anything that came to hand. It looked like a giant had furled the sail with a club, but it was safely down. Paul fired up the Kermath and I reached inside for the detailed chart of the area.

We ventured into a little bay marked three and a half fathoms and sand on the chart. The nearer we got, the smoother the water—what a relief! Doing our usual routine of me hanging over the bow in my best radar position with Paul minding the helm and the sounder, we pulled into shelter, slowed to a stop and lowered the anchor. The seagulls must have thought we were loony as we danced a jig on the foredeck that ended with a hug and a kiss.

Soon the little stove was hot enough to boil what was left in the kettle for coffee. I cooked scrambled eggs laced with smoked salmon, which we ate with the last of the rye bread before collapsing into bed. Paul slept until four in the afternoon, because he had been on watch through much of the night. But I woke at midday, refreshed, and set about collecting some of the rainwater that was thundering down on the awning. Within an hour, two ice-cream buckets full of delicious fresh water sat out on the back deck. Inside the boat the fire crackled away, so I heated up a big pan of seawater and did 24 hours' worth of dirty dishes while a potato simmered in a couple of cups of sweet rainwater. It was time to set a pan of bread rising, and a boiled mashed potato would make it extra moist and flavourful. I had to disturb Paul's head because his pillow covered the hatch where the rye flour was stored, but he barely opened his eyes. Our favourite Swedish limpa bread was soon mixed and set to rise, so I traded places with Paul. I have never experienced a more euphoric drift into sleep in all my life.

As I wrote up the story of this journey some 20-odd years later, I learned that Gillen Harbour, which we bypassed for the shelter of Rennison Island, is a beautiful haven and is still virtually empty of cruising boats—a rarity nowadays. Areas farther south, such as the Broughton Archipelago, are littered with fish farms. It is in the interest of these farms to block entry to the bays and shelters they have chosen to occupy, but it means cruisers no longer enjoy the delights of sheltered anchorages, clean water and beaches to stroll and explore that bought us so much pleasure and such good food to eat. The proliferation of these lucrative enterprises has also affected the area closer to Prince Rupert, so the bay near Kitkatla, where we found sanctuary when our forestay broke, is no longer

Storm clouds rage beyond June and Paul's safe, sheltered anchorage at Rennison Island at the end of a 24-hour-long crossing of Hecate Strait.

available. Many smart skippers buy humongous boats and head to Alaska, where fish farms are banned. But as they hasten north, few pause to enjoy the beauty of such places as Gillen Harbour. I am sorry that we, too, missed this treasure of a bay.

19 BIRTHDAY BERRIES

We enjoyed a lazy morning after crossing from the Charlottes. It was time to slow down and enjoy the bays and passageways between here and home. The beach at our anchorage on Rennison Island yielded a decent haul of firewood but no other collectibles, because fisherfolk had spent harbour days here for many years. We did enjoy stretching our legs, and our little sailboat looked serene, floating at anchor after the previous day's adventure had tested us to the limit.

Treasures such as this little bay are scattered here and there along this coast. Once we passed the entryway, the fringe of trees on the low-lying island had provided just enough of a screen to offer shelter from the gale that had ripped seaweed from rocks and tossed logs high on the outer shore. Places farther south, like Rebecca Spit on Quadra Island, provide a similar refuge. At one moment you are battered almost beyond endurance; then your boat suddenly stands upright, and you can breathe without gasping for air. We were grateful to our Norwegian fisherman and other folk along the way who had helped us mark our chart with little hand-drawn anchors and arrows. These grubby charts become more precious than gold when disaster threatens.

A fisherman we talked to at Rennison Island had told us there was a good source of drinking water in Evinrude Inlet on Princess Royal Island. This oasis was only about 10 miles away, so we hung the usual fishing line over the stern and set out to enjoy the jaunt. The southeast wind reappeared but had moderated enough to make sailing a pleasure, and since saving fuel was again a necessity, the breeze was a welcome visitor. What should have been a three-hour trip extended far beyond that, because we were facing an opposing current, and also because each time we were about to tack, a fish would strike the lure, causing a flurry of activity on deck. Fortunately most of these babies were too small to keep, so Paul released them, but he could not resist trying again for a large one. A nine-pound spring salmon struck just as we turned to enter the bay. It was a keeper, and with the line safely back on the reel and nothing left to distract us, we sailed right into the inlet.

There was a big log tethered near a rusty abandoned donkey engine with a large black hose hanging down nearby just waiting for our arrival. The stream of water gushing from the hose nearly knocked me off the deck. At one time, according to my cousin Rod, sources of fresh water were located about every 20 miles along the coast so that the old steam tugs could keep their boilers supplied. With steam tugs no longer in use but the fishing industry still active, either the Fisheries department or the fishermen themselves now cared for these hoses. Judging by the red lettering on the rock face above the hose, this one was last maintained by the Fisheries patrol vessel *Babine Post* in 1978. We were grateful for the service, and I hope that someone looks after it these days for the few thirsty folk like ourselves still roaming around in small boats with even smaller water tanks.

Evinrude Inlet was memorable because of the hordes of blackflies that emerged at dusk to make life a misery. Pity the poor sweaty loggers who worked in the woods, ran the donkey engine and arranged log booms here in earlier days. Out of habit, I scooped up salt water for doing the dishes and was startled by how warm it was. Although the chart gave no indication of land heights or lakes at the head of the bay, it is likely that the feeder stream wandered through low-lying brush and was not fed by any glaciers. It was a well-sheltered anchorage, so we had a quiet night under our netting draped over the companionway and across the hatch above our heads. Blackflies, at least, have the decency to go about their work without talking about it.

Now that our water problem was solved, we faced the need for gasoline. We had travelled many miles since the last fill-up at Tasu on the outer coast of Moresby Island. Our best bet was Klemtu. The storage tanks there had been empty on our way upcoast, but we hoped that problem had been solved in the interval. Meyers Passage, just 20-odd miles southeast of us, cut inland between Princess Royal and Swindle islands, with Klemtu located on the far side of Swindle. We had a detailed chart for the passage, and the currents through the narrows were reported in the tide book, so this looked like an easy jaunt.

We left Evinrude in the early morning with the mainsail up and the engine just ticking over. Ripples on the surface of Laredo Channel suggested the arrival of another southeast breeze, which might allow us to stretch out the fuel supply with a little help from the wind. We looked forward to seeing more new country, and I loved the challenge of sorting through the *Coast Pilot* and the current tables to plan a line of approach. By the time we arrived at the entrance, about 1:30 p.m., we were getting a nice breeze to fill the sails and the motor had been taking a rest.

"Let's do this one under sail, Paul," I suggested. "It'll be much more interesting, and the minimal current will be helping us along."

"Suits me, June," he replied. "You're the navigator. With the motor running, we'd have more control bucking the current, but if you think we can handle it, let's go."

It was fun. The sails were rigged wing and wing, and no unexpected side drafts disturbed their shape. We zipped through the narrow part, made the turn and with the genoa now pulled to the lee side, sailed into little McRae Cove, where a tumbling stream came down from a tiny lake just a short hike up the hill. After stopping for a snack, we rowed ashore with towels, soap and clean underwear in a knapsack. We found trails by the stream with loaded blueberry and huckleberry bushes on all sides. Needless to say, we munched our way up to the lake.

An industrious beaver had fallen trees to build a small dam, and the result of this effort was a series of tiny, deep pools that had Paul drooling. "Wouldn't my brother Ralph just love to drop a fish hook in there," he mused as he peered into the depths.

The sun was almost gone when we reached the lake, and the shoreline was treacherous and slippery with brown silky growth, so we clambered back down alongside the stream until we reached a rough pool that had been shaped out of fallen rocks. I would not be surprised if Natives, or maybe loggers in later years, had made this spa, for that was what it became after Paul shifted a few boulders. The water temperature was bearable, especially after we became accustomed to it, and baths were something we craved enough that a little discomfort was worth the price for becoming clean once more.

There was more salmon on hand than we could use without wasting it, so the last chore of the day was a canning session. Paul started the fire and then climbed into the rowboat in search of wood while I stayed on board to load jars with slices of the beautiful orange flesh. I was almost finished with the task when an exhausted Paul finally came back. He'd had to cut each piece of wood from dead evergreen branches with his small pruning saw instead of gathering driftwood from a beach. Ah, the joys of living a primitive life.

It was raining in the morning, with a fitful breeze to make life chilly. I pulled the anchor, because I needed to learn to do this task in case Paul ever became incapacitated. I have always believed that the first mate should be able to handle all aspects of running a boat in case of emergencies, and I had not yet mastered this chore. I managed to get the anchor and retrieval line onto the deck and lashed down properly in place. Then we hauled up the mainsail. Paul never wanted to start the engine until the line was safely coiled and secured on deck for fear that the propeller would turn over and foul it, but when he tried to get things going this time, nothing happened. I said, "You work down there and I'll sail us out of this bay so that we don't have to mess with that anchor again."

He had already figured out that the problem was in the ignition, so I held one end of a tarp over the companionway to keep out the raindrops and steered with the other hand, while he struggled to change spark plugs and fiddled with the condenser. Something worked, because the engine finally coughed and muttered before settling down to a steady hum. One of the good results of my competitive racing had been the confidence that you did not need an engine if you were prepared to be patient. I loved the challenge of moving a sailboat from point A to point B with just the power of the wind. And there were times when that skill came in handy.

When we arrived at Klemtu, we were relieved to find plenty of fuel. The freight boat with fresh groceries would be arriving later that day, but one look at the store prices convinced us that what we had on hand, either dried, canned or powdered, would suffice until we reached Namu.

Klemtu will stand out in our minds as one of the few places in which we saw other cruising boats. Just as we were ready to leave, two old-style cruisers from Prince Rupert pulled into the float. Both boats had the graceful lines that separate time-tested hulls from the shoeboxes that roll off today's production lines. One was a sleek double-ender, while the other had a square transom. We had a brief word with the owners before they climbed the steep ramp that led to the boardwalk, and learned that they often travelled as a team and were also heading to Namu. We waved goodbye and headed out into the rainy southeaster, wondering if the sun would ever shine on us again.

Once we cleared the lower end of Klemtu Channel, it was an easy reach across to the entrance of Jackson Passage that led to Mathieson Channel. Since it was already past two o'clock in the afternoon, we planned an early stop at Rescue Bay, which formed a welcome notch at the far end of the narrows. Certainly the name sounded comforting, and these two dripping travellers could do with a bit of that.

The two old-timers from Klemtu passed us in Jackson Passage and were well settled at anchor before we were able to furl our wet sails, fire up the engine and locate a spot to drop the hook.

Fortunately it was a generous harbour with lots of room for everyone. After getting the awning in place and going below to struggle out of our wet clothes, we heard a knock on the hull. One of the skippers had rowed over to invite us to after-dinner coffee on his cruiser. Since we had just completed six weeks of drinking pseudo-coffee in instant form and spent just as many days with only ourselves for company, we leapt at the offer.

The older boat had been built in 1913 by a pair of Japanese boat builders who used local wood, mostly yellow cedar. It had been made for Dr. Cade of Prince Rupert, hence the boat's name, *Edac*. In the mid-1960s, Noel and Alberta Woodworth bought the tired old-timer, rebuilt much of the dry-rotted superstructure and added a stand-up cabin. The results were pleasing to the eye. The younger craft had probably been built in the 1930s. These venerable old cruisers had shared many adventures.

Unlike our boat, *Edac* boasted a stove with a good-sized oven that was put to regular use. Alberta told us they had picked pails full of wild blueberries that she had turned into pies. When they landed at Klemtu, she had taken loaves of bread from the oven and stored them, along with two pies, in the cupboard on the back deck to cool down so they would be ready for eating at lunchtime. When she and Noel finished their shopping and returned to the boat, they discovered the cupboard had been torn open and all that remained of her work was blueberry paw-marks on the back deck. The horde of hungry hounds had struck again!

Even without a taste of the berry pies, we thoroughly enjoyed our visit, swapping tales of anchoring horrors, hot-springs pleasures and other boating adventures while lounging on soft seats in a warm, dry cabin, drinking great coffee and sampling Alberta's excellent cookies. There is a special ambience in a wooden hull. The walls do not drip with condensation, and the sound of waves is muted as they slap gently on the hull. Wooden boats are not as roomy as fibreglass ones because the ribs, longitudinal timbers and bracing take up valuable inner space. Yet these older boats seem to abound in storage lockers and hidden spaces under the floorboards that provide hidey-holes for many treasures. Layers of paint or spar varnish give an enamelled finish to inner surfaces that glow with the golden light from the usual oil lanterns.

When the evening drew to a close, we faced the reality of a chilly row back to *Wood Duck*, where the fire had long since died down; but it was our summer home, so we climbed contentedly into our bed in the forepeak to keep each other warm. It was a nice ending to a companionable evening. It seemed fitting that all three boats in that safe remote harbour were wooden ones from earlier years. There were no generators humming to break the stillness of the night, just the sound of wavelets slapping the hull to remind us that we were waterfolk.

August 16 was Paul's birthday. The new pair of rugby trousers that I had hidden away under the bunk would make a useful present. Now I would be able to wash both his pairs of pants, which were just about ready to stand on their own. Laundry facilities had been seriously lacking ever since Tasu, although I'd have gladly soaked our clothes in a stream and pounded them on a rock if there had been any way to get them dry again.

Liberated women of today might well ask how it was that I was washing Paul's clothes for him, but when you consider his struggle to cut firewood and keep both the fire and the old engine running, it is easy to see why I felt that food preparation and laundry were my roles along with navigation and sailing.

We agreed to celebrate his birthday at anchor that evening so spent most of the day slogging along behind Dowager and Lady Douglas islands, down through Mathieson Channel, Perceval Narrows and Reid Passage before reaching Seaforth Channel, which would lead us inland to Bella Bella. Late in the afternoon we decided to take a break and try our luck hunting for stove wood near Idol Point Light. A small bay opened up just west of the light, and the shoreline looked promising in the binoculars. Once we pulled in there, we were out of any wind, although boat traffic could set up a wake, but our need to harvest wood was greater than our fear of being pooped by waves.

The beach held little in the way of drift logs, but we scrabbled around until we managed to fill two onion sacks with a motley collection of soggy bits of fuel. Paul suggested we take a look back in the forest in case there were downed trees with knots that we could kick loose. Eight paces in from the shoreline, we found bushes with the biggest blueberries I have ever seen. They would put the commercial variety to shame. This part of Dufferin Island is flat and boggy, with streams rattling brownish water out across the fine gravel every quarter mile along the shoreline.

We ate until we could hold no more, never once thinking that we were probably stealing the crop belonging to one of the local Native families. Since both of us came from a society that uses fences instead of tradition to protect our "farms," it didn't occur to us that we were likely trespassing. And, who knows? Given that the local Bella Bella store carried everything from bananas to McGavin's white bread, maybe no one ever came these days to harvest this wonderful patch of berries. In times past the air would have been filled with the happy chatter of women's and children's voices competing with the calls of hungry birds who also valued these treasures.

I have since learned that the "owners" of a particular mountain berry patch would burn the bushes in the fall to clear away dead branches and encourage new growth. The plants grew stronger with the ash added to the soil. A patch like that would lie fallow for a few years as it replaced the burned-off branches, so a group or family would burn the various patches it was entitled to in rotation. These blazes would occasionally get out of control, and when commercial loggers claimed ownership of these mountain areas, government agents probably chased the Native berry farmers off the land. Closer to the shore, where they could access food-bearing crops more easily, women dug holes around the plants and filled them with scraps of offal, crushed clamshells, ashes from their fires, and seaweed. In short, they took care of their food-producing plants, including crabapples and berries. We latter-day pioneers on the BC coast, of which I consider myself one, are so pleased with ourselves when we carry out these farming practices in our carefully fenced gardens, never once thinking that we did not, indeed, invent organic gardening.

Women also grew and tended root crops in the naturally fertile soil on the flat land of river estuaries. Indigenous plants like Pacific silverweed, northern rice-root, springbank clover, camas lilies, Nootka Lupine and wapato produced bigger and sweeter roots when they were cultivated by hand, weeded, replanted and improved by moving desirable specimens in from other areas. Given that root crops were such a valuable part of their diet and that suitable land on which to grow this food was scarce, it is no wonder that Natives responded with hostility when White farmers came to the coast and promptly fenced in the estuaries for grazing cattle and making hay. These areas had been the preserve of particular Native families since the beginning of time, where they could grow plants to eat or trade for other goods.

But all this history of ownership was obviously not worrying us in 1983. Had we known, we wouldn't have been so greedy, although the amount we munched in half an hour hardly put a dent in the berry supply on those healthy bushes. Two dozen robins could have eaten more in half the time.

The rain that had held off while we were onshore returned with a vengeance, so we heaved our sacks of wet firewood into the rowboat, hurried back to our watery home, stowed the dripping mess under the seats in the cockpit and sailed off the anchorage. We encountered a large ferro-cement sailboat going in our direction, and, of course, I could not resist making it into a kind of mini-race. Paul got enthusiastic as well, so we moved along as briskly as possible, running with the wind that came blowing in from the Pacific Ocean right on our tail. It was hardly a fair race given that *Wood Duck* was such a sleek little 26-footer carrying way too much sail and the Sampson-designed boat was someone's sturdy home.

We aimed for Ormindale Harbour, just around the corner from Bella Bella, because it looked like a good bet for the night. We got there shortly before the ketch and anchored in the lee of the shore, well into the bay. There was even enough left of the day to give me time to plan a birthday dinner.

When I rummaged through the cooking supplies stored under the starboard seat, I found I was out of baking powder. There went the pineapple/walnut birthday cake. But I did find some dried squash that my father-in-law had prepared in his food dehydrator, along with other delicious goodies like dried banana fingers and apple slices. *Recipes for a Small Planet* suggested using squash in a casserole dish, so that was going to have to stand in for a cake. We cracked rock crabs, had a salad consisting of shredded cabbage, carrots and the sprouts that Paul had grown on board, ate the casserole and washed it all down with sake warmed in a pot of water on the stove. Even the candle stuck in the middle of the squash casserole didn't look too silly. This was indeed a birthday dinner to remember!

20 CLAMS AND HALIBUT

Next morning we slept in until eight. Usually we were up and on our way by that time, but Namu, where we could top up the fuel tank, wash our clothes and get a meal, was not far away. When we got there, the supply boat was just unloading, though we found the prices in the store were much higher than before. Also, to our disappointment, the commissary where we usually ate was closed. When we asked the woman in the liquor store about this tragedy, she said it was one of several cutbacks BC Packers, which owned Namu, had put in place. The company no longer processed fish at the plant—it was cheaper to ship the catch to Prince Rupert or plants farther south. The only remaining employees at Namu were couples who occupied the small houses on-site and did their own cooking. The Namu Hilton dormitory was closed, as were most of the other services.

The laundress said she was not allowed to do our washing, partly because some of the machines no longer worked, so we stopped in at the café on the large dock nearby to discuss our troubles with the woman running that concession. She fixed us a couple of milkshakes and told us that she would do our laundry for us on the quiet that evening if we brought it up when we came to have dinner. We almost hugged her before hurrying back to our boat to gather up our stinky load.

When we returned to the café at 6:30 p.m., it was closed, but the cook heard our knock, let us in the side door and proceeded to make us dinner. While we munched away, she put our things in the washer, and we enjoyed a visit with her. She was a widow, about 50 years old. Her husband had been a commercial fisherman out of Pender Harbour, so she knew old Harry Dusenbury, who had worked on my dad's boat engine years earlier. She said that Harry's son Roy, and Roy's wife, Doris, still lived at Pender Harbour. It is a small coast, after all.

Next morning we breakfasted at the café, got our sweet-smelling laundry from the cook and prepared to continue our journey home. We were sad to leave Namu in its rapidly diminishing state. This cannery had served us well on our coastal trips, and we knew things would only deteriorate with the passing years. Company towns that rely on a single resource rise and fall all over the western world. Now this small outport was joining others such as Ocean Falls and Tasu. No wonder new large cruising boats were being built with showers, freezers, washers and dryers, garbage compacters and the generators necessary to run these appliances. No wonder they fill anchorages with fumes and sound and take up huge amounts of dock space when they choose to tie up for the night.

A gentle northwest wind carried us steadily down toward Darby Channel, which marks the upcoast edge of Rivers Inlet. When we arrived, we found the area swarming with small sport-fishing skiffs from nearby lodges that cater to people who fly in for a few days while they strive to catch the biggest fish of their lives. Sometimes, given the limits placed on them by fishing regulations, they have been known to keep their catch until near the end of the day, when they throw the smaller fish back in the water, to the delight of eagles and seals who monitor their activities. Paul could not resist trying his luck and, as usual, hooked a respectable-sized salmon.

We motored around into the shelter provided by the Penrose Islands. It was really hot, so off came our clothes. When Paul finished gutting the fish I persuaded him to hold it up in front like a loincloth while I took his picture. We both had a good laugh when the photo was developed because it was clear that he got a thrill out of hooking such a large fish. We decided this fish should be lightly smoked and put into jars for the winter, so after it was cut up we sprinkled it with a minimal amount of salt and went off to find a wood supply. Paul needed green alder to provide smoke, and I volunteered to search for firewood.

The white beach looked so inviting that I left my shoes in the rowboat and set off barefoot. What a painful error! Instead of ground-up clamshells, I was treading on shards of broken barnacles that were as sharp as the day they were harvested by hungry Natives. On this part of the coast, the common type of barnacle is the size of a St. Bernard in comparison to the Chihuahua-sized barnacle of the lower coast. Many are larger than a big coffee mug and are filled with edible meat, similar to that of a snail. When cooked, the contents look like scrambled eggs. The broken shells of these beasties were not only sharp, but also reflected brilliant sunlight off the slightly convex surfaces, casting up enough glare to make me squint. I struggled blindly along the shore and found little in the way of usable fuel, but while I was away, the bedding draped over the rigging got well baked by the hot sun, so some good came of my foray.

The weather remained hot. It was a wonderful treat after our damp summer prowling the upper coast and the Queen Charlotte Islands, so we meandered along, sampling one bay after another. We passed Cape Caution, helped along by a gentle breeze from the southwest. When things got a little livelier, we sought shelter in the Walker Group, a cluster of small islands just northeast of Port Hardy, about midway across the channel between Vancouver Island and the mainland. The only cruising information I had was from John Chappell's book *Cruising Beyond Desolation Sound*, which said "An anchorage has been suggested between Staples and Kent Islands."

Next morning, since we had no need of supplies at Port Hardy, we decided to make use of what was now only a moderate breeze and cross over to Blunden Harbour on the mainland just downcoast from our present location. The *Wood Duck* appreciated the breeze, and the bright sunshine made for a sparkling day. We anchored in front of the old village site in the inner harbour, because Paul wanted to harvest some wood for lathe work from a dead yew tree that he remembered seeing there on our previous visit. The tree had solid knots and a beautifully gnarled shape but, oh, was it tough. We took turns sawing away with Paul's little pruning saw, which had served us so well that summer. Finally the tree fell. Paul trimmed off a few remaining branches and lugged the trunk down to the beach. We towed the six-foot-long section to the boat, hoisted it aboard with the main halyard and the winch, and Paul lashed it down on the side deck.

By the time we caught our breath, we noticed that the wind had returned and was beginning to slew the boat from one side to the other. "Paul," I said, "I've been looking at the chart, and I think we'd be safer in the Raynor Group of islands just downcoast from here. There's one tall enough to deflect the wind, with about six fathoms of water in which to anchor."

"Let's go, then," he replied. "I'd rather not stay here if we're going to drag during the night." So we sailed off the anchorage and out of the harbour, paused to set a crab pot near the big stream that flowed down from the mainland shore, then aimed for the quiet water behind the island. By the time we were well hooked and were on our way below, we noticed a small orange fishing boat, the *Betty K*, swing in through the other entrance and drop its hook nearby. The fisherman waited for one of us to come back up on deck and then called out to offer us a fish. I traded him some fresh fruit for three small salmon that I decided to pickle for a change. I had lemons, onions, spices, rock salt and vinegar, so was all set up for that chore. The results were always appreciated and tasted not unlike pickled herring, but not as greasy or as chewy.

In the morning, after we checked the local shoreline for abalone and found none, Paul rowed us over to the trap, where we found the biggest Dungeness crab we had ever seen. This anchorage was obviously begging us to stay for a while. On our way back to the boat, we spotted clam squirts coming up from the beach near the boat, so I told Paul, "I'm going to get a few clams. It'll make a nice change of diet for us. Take me back to the boat for the little rake and a sack, and I'll go digging while you get the fire started for breakfast."

The clams were certainly there. There wasn't much of a beach exposed among the rock outcroppings, but it was jam-packed with old-fashioned littleneck clams. I dug a few dozen, scrubbed them with seaweed in salt water, loaded them into the onion sack, then squelched my way back to the dinghy. When I got back to the boat, I hung them over the side in the ocean so they could expel the sand that lurked inside the shells, ready to surprise unwary munchers.

If the tide had been lower, I could have dug for larger, more flavourful butter clams. Both pioneers and Natives preferred them over the smaller littlenecks. These big clams were so full of meat they could not even close their shells. Native cooks put butter and razor clams on a bed of seaweed in a firepit on the beach, and then covered the lot to cook in the steam, not unlike a New England clambake. The women would string the steamed clam meat on yew sticks and stand them around a smoky fire to preserve them for winter use. Once they were dried, these chewy, protein-rich morsels were stored, ready to be added to the cooking pot on cold, wet, winter nights when clam digging would have been a miserable chore. The women also preserved cockles, because the long, chewy necks on these unusual clams made tasty soothers for cranky babies.

Each clan had its traditional clam beds. Family members would pick rocks out of the sand and move them down toward the water, forming a dike that helped level the area. Judith Williams has researched and photographed these structures and written about them in a delightful little book, *Clam Gardens*. Unfortunately, the area where I was harvesting was too far up the beach to hold butter clams, which live deeper in the sand and farther down the beach than the littlenecks. As well, with the curse of red tide, which seems more prevalent these days, the big clams are usually left alone because they hold the fatal toxins for much longer than the small variety do.

Back at the boat after a late breakfast, I checked the pantry. The storage bin under the settee held canned tomatoes, herbs like basil, and powdered Japanese soup stock, so bouillabaisse was an easy one-pot meal. We were out of bread, but otherwise life was good. "Paul," I said, "I was thinking that maybe I could bake a nice rye loaf, make some bouillabaisse with a handful of those clams, a bit of crab and some rock cod, and then we could invite the fisherman over to share our dinner. I'm feeling a little guilty about accepting three salmon from him for just a few pieces of fruit, so I'll go fishing while the bread rises."

In the early 1980s, before rockfish were harvested commercially on this coast, it was easy to catch as many as you needed simply by jigging with a little diamond-shaped lead weight called a Buzz Bomb. These came in a great array of colours, designed more to catch the eye of the fisherman than to intrigue the fish. What mattered was the action of the lure. It had to look like injured prey as it tumbled and fell near the rocky incline of the shore. I set off in the rowboat with a rusty pair of pump pliers for getting the hook loose, wooden oars and a fishing rod equipped with the little magic lure. Because I had done this so many times before, I didn't bother to take along a knife.

I was happy to be out on the water with a fishing rod in my hands, even though the overcast sky and some cloudy spawn in the water made for poor visibility as I peered into the depths. Before long I had one small rock cod in the boat and set to work catching another. The second one was slow in coming, but it hit with an impressive jerk. The line sizzled off the reel and the rod tip bent down into the water. I set up the drag to slow things down and managed to crank in about three feet before the fish pulled it back out. "Man oh man, what have I got here?" I muttered to myself. "I'm in 18 feet of water. There are no herring about, so it can't be a spring salmon. But it sure is strong, whatever it is."

My pulse raced as I puffed away, muttering all the while. After a long struggle, the fish relaxed and slowly floated to the surface. I peered into the murky water and saw a sight that made me pray for something I could use to cut the line. Out of the depths loomed a great grey, mottled shape that paused for a moment before rolling over to expose a pale green underside. Then, with one vigorous flop, a monster of a halibut righted itself and drifted back down to the seabed from whence it came.

My eyes bugged out. I gave a horrified yelp and then the tug-of-war resumed. When my arms felt as though they would pull out of their sockets, the fish finally gave up and a new dilemma emerged. Who was going to hold the rod while I rowed the boat back to the sailboat? I decided to jam the rod between my bottom and the seat and clamp the reel between my knees. I carefully turned the dinghy around so I could tow the fish behind me. Every so often the beast would sound and I would grab the rod out from under me and go through the whole process again, all the while muttering, "Oh dear, oh dear, oh dear!" By the time I was around the point of land and could see the sailboat, sweat was dripping off the end of my nose and running down my shirtfront. I yelled, "Paul, help! I'm in trouble here." Goodness knows how he was going to help, with me in the dinghy and him on the boat, but I was exhausted and getting desperate.

Paul heard me coming and stuck his head up through the hatch. "I was just about to pull up the anchor and come looking for you," he called.

"Oh, Paul, I've caught a halibut and I can't let it go." Puffing my way to the boat, I lifted my hip, grabbed the rod and handed it to him. What a relief! Of course the fish, after that nice rest, sounded again, so Paul was stuck with the task of saving his rod while I tied the dinghy forward, out of the way. Then we stood out on the stern of the boat, beyond the rigging, with the rod bending in a U-shape each time the fish thrashed and headed for the bottom of the sea.

"What are we going to do with it, Paul? That's a lot of fish for two people to eat."

"Well I'm sure not going to let it go," he replied. "I've hauled many a fish over the gunwales of this boat but never a halibut, and I surely do love halibut steaks. We'll eat some, can some and give the rest away." He alternately reeled it in and let it run out while we discussed what to do next.

"Don't try to bring it on board while it's still alive, Paul. My brother told me that when they thrash about, they're strong enough to break up your cockpit."

"Well, we don't have a gun to shoot him. I'll have to try bleeding him to death. Just give me a minute to get into the dinghy so I can reach him without falling into the chuck." He handed me the fishing gear and scrambled over the side with the hunting knife and the little hatchet he used for chopping wood. While I held the rod up high and steered the reluctant captive in his direction, he stabbed away, trying to kill it. Each time Paul attacked, the fish splashed mightily before sounding again—slash, stab, slash, stab—with me struggling to reel it back in and bring it within range. Paul was finally able to make contact with the axe and got some blood flowing, but by this time he was thoroughly soaked with water flung up by the thrashing of the fish as it fought to get away. "I hope the local dogfish are all away. I'd hate to lose this beauty to a bunch of those hungry sharks."

"Maybe our luck will hold," I said. "But I am worried about this fragile line. Maybe we'd better secure him with the cod jig." While Paul held the rod, I managed to thread the big triple hooks down into the gill cavity. Then I tied off the coarse line to a cleat. "How about a glass of wine and we'll wait to see what happens." I plopped down on the seat.

Glasses of wine eventually morphed into a light supper of newly baked bread and cheese, while the poor halibut slowly drained his life force into the ocean. I sighed, "It seems like a lingering sort of painful murder, doesn't it? No wonder the fishermen use a gun. But perhaps we would feel better if we look at it from a Native point of view and thank the halibut for coming up out of the ocean to feed us."

"We'd better see if it's ready to join us on board," said Paul as he gathered up the plates and wineglasses and carried them down into the cabin. "It'll be getting dark soon, and we still have to gut it and cut it up for safe storage until we find some more canning jars. We should be able to buy some at Alert Bay on our way downcoast."

There was no way we could lift this huge fish over the gunwale by hand, so Paul decided to use the mainsail boom and the topping lift, along with the big gaff hook I had found that summer on a beach on the outer coast. Some unlucky commercial fisherman had lost his grip on it. He had carefully repaired a crack in the handle, binding it with sturdy cod-line, so no doubt he said a few bad words as it slipped from his grasp. I do not know if fishermen count such tools as their lucky talisman, but I surely felt lucky the day I stumbled upon it amongst the driftwood.

Paul tied one end of a line to the handle of the gaff and drove the angled barb clear through the fish just behind its head. It was a lucky thing we had that sturdy hook—anything smaller would have been useless. It served its purpose admirably as Paul tied the free end of the line to the boom, including his heavy-duty scale in the rig. After much grunting and cranking on the winch, we got the halibut clear of the water. The gauge on the scale teetered between 62 and 63 pounds, so it must have been a male fish. I swung the boom in over the boat, and we carefully lowered our burden onto the deck, placing it dark side down as we had been advised at the small logging camp on the Charlottes.

June caught this huge halibut while fishing in shallow water. She was in the rowboat using a small buzz bomb as a lure.

Once the lines and mess were cleared away, Paul sat down to hone his battered knife. "Since I can't help you right now," I said, "I'd better go ashore while there is still enough light and find more fuel for our stove. We're going to need lots if we decide to can any of this monster."

I chuckled on my return to the boat when I found him naked as he wielded his knife. "Good grief, man, why the striptease?"

"My clothes were soaked from the halibut battle, and I'm darned if I want to get my clean outfit all bloody, so I decided to take everything off." He told me that the halibut's gut was full of little beach crabs, so that was what this old boy had been eating in the shallow water when he unwisely bit my hook. It was dark by the time Paul finished the chore, so we wrapped the fish pieces carefully and stored them next to the water tank under the bunk.

The next day we bought two dozen pint jars at Alert Bay, Paul gave away halibut steaks to all comers and I set to work bottling the fish. The texture and flavour proved to be a tad disappointing, but library cookbooks came to the rescue, and canned halibut became the major ingredient of casserole dishes during the wintertime.

21 THE JOURNEY HOME

Our summer holidays were coming to an end, so we reluctantly left the Broughton Archipelago and pointed *Wood Duck's* nose in the direction of Seymour Narrows. En route we made the usual stop at Port Neville, powering out of that sheltered spot next morning and fishing the back eddies because the current was running against us. In every nook and cranny there was a seine boat moored bow and stern across the gap, guarding its favourite area while the fishermen waited for the opening of a salmon fishery at six o'clock on Sunday evening. As for us, we put in a long tiring day. I became totally fed up with the whole routine of poking along, trying to catch yet another fish, partly because it was my job to stand by the mast and watch for shallows that might foul our lines. With no shelter from the cold, rain-splattering breeze and no chance to sit down, it was neither restful nor pleasant, yet I felt it was my duty to protect the hull and equipment from damage. How I longed to just drop the anchor in a small bay and read the day away in the warmth of the cabin until the time came to make a dash for the narrows at slack tide. My lack of enthusiasm was directly attributable to a cold that had my nose dripping and my lungs complaining.

The day wore on and by tea time we were anchored at Turn Island. The next morning's logbook entry said: *Departed Turn Island at 0900 hrs. Current changes in our favour at 1500 hrs.* That meant one more tedious day of fishing the shoreline past all the waiting seiners on our way to Seymour Narrows. It rained bullets and was blowing a howler of a southeaster, yet we poked along, fishing and occasionally losing a salmon—a totally discouraging sort of day.

I became thoroughly chilled and ached in every joint, so I begged off, deserted my post and crawled into bed. Paul could do what he liked. I no longer cared. At that point it would have been a wise decision to head into a place like Granite Bay, but I was too sick to be assertive, and he was so determined to catch a big fish to share with his friends that he could not quit. So he pressed on into the mouth of the waiting dragon.

He told me later that he finally pulled in his line just before three o'clock, five miles short of the narrows. By the time he reached them, the current was pushing him along so fast that he shot right through and within half an hour was down by the pulp mill south of the narrows. As he moved out past the shelter of Race Point, the southeast wind began making itself known, building up sharper and steeper waves as it met the ever-increasing force of the current. Although he had the throttle fully open, Paul said there were times when the wind gusted so hard that the hull was stopped and he lost steering control. Meanwhile, the current was carrying the boat inexorably toward Campbell River. Paul had a sudden vision of little *Wood Duck* being swept past the harbour entrance and out into the raging turmoil off Cape Mudge.

His frantic voice roused me like a fire alarm. "June, June, get up here, I can't watch for the harbour entrance and handle the boat at the same time. I need you." I was horrified by what I saw. Had the boat been under sail, we would have had little canvas up and would be tacking back and forth across Discovery Passage, still in control. As it was, the small Kermath was doing its best, but that was not enough. When the boat crested a wave and dove down into the abyss, forward progress was stalled. As the hull rose again into the air, the wind tried to force it off to one side. Fortunately we were almost at the harbour mouth, so when a slight lull arrived, Paul was able to point the bow in the right direction. The sudden peace as we rounded into the shelter of the breakwater left us both gasping.

We pulled on damp, clean clothes, locked up the poor boat and went to have dinner at the Discovery Inn. As luck would have it, their Sunday special was chicken smorgasbord, so although the place was packed, we did not have to wait to be served. We grabbed plates, piled on the food and sat down to a meal cooked by somebody else and eaten at a table that stayed still. I had little appetite, but appreciated the draft-free warmth of the place.

When we got back to our wet boat, Paul lit a good hot fire and crawled into bed while I hung clothing up to dry. Then I sat and nursed a cup of hot tea as I thought about the misadventures of the day. I could tell that Paul was upset with the way things had gone because he was quiet all evening. I am sure that he had felt abandoned. Also, he may have finally realized the extreme danger we were facing. Had the engine quit with no sail ready, we would have been swept past the mouth of the harbour and out past Cape Mudge to meet the rollers that have built up strength as they move up the Strait of Georgia. That, coupled with the shallows off the point and the force of the opposing tide, is deadly. In those conditions the Cape has claimed many boats and even more lives.

I should have insisted that we seek shelter instead of leaving him to plunge virtually alone into such a nasty bit of water. I knew that it was foolhardy to keep on travelling in those conditions, but I was too cold and exhausted from the lung infection to be able to think of what lay ahead. Had he been comfortable as a sailor, he would have known to get the mainsail up and fully reefed if he had no choice but to proceed. However, there are times on this coast when discretion is required, and this was one of those times. There had been no pressing reason for us to be underway. I had raced my sailboat in similar conditions, but in that case I was out there because I wanted to be and because that was the day of the contest. Also, I had a well-rested, experienced crew and a well-tuned boat. *Wood Duck* was an old lady and had lived through periods of neglect. That we survived the trip to the Queen Charlotte Islands was possibly more good luck than good management. Except for the last few hours of our crossing of Hecate Strait, we had managed to sit out bad weather and had not become holed or lost during the great adventure. That we had come through this last trial was nothing short of miraculous.

And the miracles continued next day. We woke to brilliant sunshine on a windless morning. The previous day's gale was already no more than a bad memory. An eight o'clock start allowed us to slip out into a helpful current that took us to Cape Mudge in short order. Blue haze from oil-burning outboard engines almost obscured the swarm of little boats trying to catch a dwindling supply of salmon. With slack tide soon upon us, the number of boats rapidly increased as more and more of them hurried out from the various local fishing lodges. We also hung out our fishing lines, thinking it would be nice to arrive at Warren and Ginny Tormeys' place on Cortes Island with something for supper.

No one seemed to be landing anything except for one small cruiser with grandma, grandpa and one young grandson on board. The little boy reeled in his line heroically, and grandma had the net ready when out of the water popped a small grilse, a juvenile salmon. She netted it for him and looked apologetically our way while the child danced off into the cabin to show his marvellous catch to grandpa. Of course we would not rat on her for keeping an illegal fish. Who would want to squelch such joy?

Like most of the other fisherfolk that morning, we, too, were skunked, so we pulled in our lines and set out for Cortes Bay under power, with no sign of the previous day's southeast wind to help us along our way. We did pause briefly at Sutil Point, off the southwest corner of Cortes Island, but we drew a blank there too and moved over to the sandspit off the northeast corner of Hernando Island. My lure finally attracted a four-pound spring salmon. This beauty was capable of growing up to weigh 30 or 40 pounds, but we kept him anyway.

No one seemed to realize that this great resource was dwindling almost to the point of extinction. Commercial fishermen still trolled these waters, and sport fishing was a lucrative business providing a good income for the various industries that surrounded the sport—from boat and gear manufacturers, motor sales and service people to hoteliers, restaurateurs, etc. Just four years later, I saw my first deep-sea dragger tied up at the dock in Ucluelet. These boats literally scraped a net along the ocean floor, scooping up every living thing. Within a few years the old-time fishermen were complaining that they no longer found salmon feeding at the various shallow banks that had provided them with dependable catches for years. This seems strange, since the draggers were not supposed to contact these areas. But these underwater pastures of the ocean were being stripped bare of all life. And sport fishers like us were doing our share to deplete the resource as we fed ourselves on the bounty of the seas while travelling these glorious waterways.

When we arrived at the Tormeys' house, our small fish was received with delight, because they had not caught much that season. Luckily they had a full freezer and a huge vegetable garden, so they had not starved. In all the years that they had been coming north from Salem, Oregon, they had always been able to take home salmon that they had caught and canned after trolling around the area of Mary Point, but this year had been a disappointment to them. Never again would this resource be as plentiful as it had been in the early days of White settlement on the coast.

We left Cortes at midday on September 2, spent the night at Westview, near Powell River, and hurried off next morning in time for Paul to fish at slack tide near Scotch Fir Point. After catching two moderate-sized cod, we motored to Secret Cove, where we anchored for the night in a little nook near a small island. Morning greeted us with a fouled anchor line and a brisk northwest wind. Paul managed to work the chain loose, so we unfurled the genoa and were able to sail right out of the harbour, only to be met by boat after boat pulling into the bay. Several people waved to let us know there was trouble ahead. Sure enough, the Environment Canada predictions were wrong. Ahead of us we could see rollers topped by frothy whitecaps surging into the entrance to Welcome Pass.

Coastal travellers have indeed welcomed this aptly named pass, which is formed by a gap between Thormanby Island and the mainland. If you are heading upcoast and have endured a raging southeaster, you plunge through this narrow opening into quieter waters, secure in the knowledge that you will soon be in either

Secret Cove or Pender Harbour. If you are heading downcoast, as we were, you know that the pass will give you shelter for a few miles while you assess the situation. If you choose to wait it out, there are coves nearby that provide snug anchorages until things improve. We chose to go on. At least the wind would be on our tail, pushing us toward the city. We were so short of time we decided to use it to hurry us on our way. After all, our boat was meant for sailing, so we faced an exhilarating day of running downwind.

We rolled in more and more of the genoa as the day wore on and as the waves increased in size. Sparkling whitecaps sizzled up near the edge of the deck each time the swells overtook us, raised the stern, surged past and then cradled us back into the trough. It felt as though we were being rocked by an overenthusiastic nanny who swung us up, up, up and then down, down, down, but the

Running home before a sparkling westerly wind.

designer of this sweet craft knew what he was doing when he took up his pencil. There was never a moment we felt in any danger.

Sailors endure all kinds of indignities, such as being soaked and chilled on upwind beats. Often the wind, having done its mischief, takes a nap and leaves the boat rolling miserably from side to side in leftover swells, with no breeze to fill the sails and steady the hull. But sailors put up with all this knowing that eventually the rewards of a bright day and a downwind sail will erase all those bad memories and fill their hearts with joy. Toques come off, sweaters and gloves are tossed below, and cool drinks come to hand. The boat and the wind are in sync, and all is well with the world.

And so it was with us. As the day wore on, fewer and fewer boats were in evidence, just ourselves and three other sailboats, plus a huge American cruiser that wallowed past us en route to Vancouver's inner harbour. By seven in the evening I was exhausted. As great as the sailing had been, it was a relief to reach the North Arm of the Fraser River. Wind-driven waves broke in confused surges, slamming crossly into the rock jetty that protects this waterway, the first obstruction since they left the islands 30 miles upcoast. They shattered into rainbows that fanned up into a mist, then swirled away toward Spanish Banks. A few intrepid gulls rode the wind like toy kites, struggling to stay aloft as they were tossed up and then suddenly plunged downward. And we, like the gulls, surged into the quieter seas behind the breakwater with the scrap of a sail still urging us on.

Paul wanted to keep on going to his mooring upriver under the Arthur Laing Bridge, but the current was strongly against us, and I knew the wind that was pushing us forward would be affected by the landforms, so I pleaded fatigue and said we should drop anchor in Cowards Cove, where the journey had begun. This proved to be a big mistake.

During the long dark night, the winds grew to gale proportions and screamed through the rigging. Halyards hammered the mast, and the anchor line groaned under the strain. There were times we feared the nearby barges would break loose and crush us against the log booms that filled the shallows near us. We took turns going on deck with the flashlight to check our bearings, but by early morning things began to calm down and we seized a few hours of fitful sleep.

When we arose, I apologized for insisting that we anchor instead of proceeding upstream. It was sentiment that made me want one more night afloat. I knew that Paul and I would now go our separate ways, but the past summer together had been a major adventure that left both of us euphoric with the knowledge that we had undertaken a risky challenge and come through it unscathed. As we sat together over our second cup of breakfast coffee, I thanked him for trusting me with the navigation and sailing.

"But, June, I knew you were smarter than me."

"Oh no," I replied. "It took mature judgement on your part to grant me a free hand. There were things that I could do well and things about which I knew nothing. I could never have kept the engine running or done the repairs to the rigging. We did this together, with each one of us contributing what we knew best to the venture. That is what kept us alive and took this small 26-foot boat all the way to the Charlottes and back. That was teamwork at its finest. But I do have a confession to make. Had I found the time to look at those empty charts of the outer coast before we left the city, I think I would have scrubbed the entire trip. The shock of discovering how much of the area remained uncharted would have been enough to convince me that we were making a big mistake."

"But we survived, didn't we?" chuckled Paul.

"We did, but that was partly because you listened to my concerns when I felt that it was wiser to remain at anchor rather than venturing out into those uncharted waters. There were times out off the coast of Moresby Island when it felt as though we were early explorers, venturing into the great unknown. But unlike those intrepid folk, we did have charts showing landforms such as mountain shapes to guide us. And, in a pinch, the Coast Guard might have come to find us, although I would have had a hard time telling them our exact location. Much of what happened was just plain good luck, Paul, especially during our crossings of Hecate Strait."

"And we were certainly lucky in that blow last night," said Paul. "So we'd better get on our way upstream while good fortune still smiles on us."

The anchor was reluctant to abandon its sticky hold on the mud of Cowards Cove, but it finally yielded to Paul's tugging and a nudge from the Kermath engine. We turned *Wood Duck*'s bow into the current of the river and made our way upstream to face a new future, each in our own way.

GLOSSARY

beam sea: waves coming toward the side of the hull, causing the
  boat to roll from side to side
beat: the act of sailing into the wind, zigzagging upwind
boom: a metal pole attached to the mast to which the lower edge
  of the mainsail is attached
bow: the forward end of a boat
bow pulpit: a metal railing at the boat's bow
close-hauled: sailing as close into the wind direction as possible
day marker: an aid to navigation that is not necessarily lit. Indicated
  on the chart by a symbol that looks like an exclamation mark
fairlead: a turning block through which a line runs in order to
  control a sail
fetch: the distance the wind has to travel across the water
following sea: waves coming from astern
foredeck: the deck nearest the bow
foresail: any sail fastened to the bow of a boat
forestay: a cable between the bow of a boat and the top of the mast
  to provide forward support for the mast
full keel/fin keel: a keel running the full length of the hull/a keel
  like a shark's fin
genoa: a large-size foresail
gunwale: the edge of the deck
headsail: a sail that is forward of the mast; for example, a genoa
headstay: any sail fastened to the bow of the boat. There are many
  shapes and sizes available

helm: the steering device, either a tiller or a wheel. To be "at the helm" means to be in control

dragging hook: the hook is an anchor; an anchor that does not grip the ocean floor is dragging

jury-rig: to improvise a temporary or makeshift fix to replace damaged equipment

keel: a beam that runs down the middle of the ship, from bow to stern, and serves as the foundation of the ship and often projects from the bottom; "keel" also refers to this projection

kellet: a weight that is run partway down the anchor line to alter the angle of pull

knot: one nautical mile per hour

lazarette: a storage bin, usually aft on a boat

lead line: a weighted line used to determine the depth of the water

lifeline: a safety line running the length of the deck; a body harness can be clipped onto it so if a person goes overboard, he or she is still attached to the boat

lines: ropes

mainsail: the sail fastened to the mast and to the boom

main traveller: a block through which the line runs that is attached to the end of the boom

reach: a point of sail between close-hauled and running before the wind

reefing: a reef is one of several lines across a sail for taking it in or rolling it up; reefing means taking in a reef or reefs

roller furling: a form of reefing in which a sail is mechanically rolled around a line (for example, the headsail can be rolled around the headstay) to reduce the amount of cloth exposed to the wind

running before the wind: to sail with the wind rather than against it

sheerline: the shape of the deck edge as it runs from bow to stern

sheets: the lines tied to a sail

slop: lumpy, irregular waves

stern: the rear part of a boat

tack: heading off in the opposite direction to the flow of the wind tiller: a wooden bar used to turn the rudder

towing bit: a sturdy, T-shaped fastening on the front deck to which a towing line can be tied

trip line: a rope tied to the head of the anchor that will help dislodge it if it catches on an obstruction

way on: moving through the water as opposed to sitting still

whisker pole: a light, portable pole used to hold the trailing corner of a headsail away from the hull when running before the wind

BIBLIOGRAPHY

Anderson, Doris. *Evergreen Islands.* Sidney, BC: Gray's Publishing, 1979.

Anderson, Flo. *Lighthouse Chronicles.* Madeira Park, BC: Harbour Publishing, 1998.

Blackman, Margaret B. *During My Time.* Vancouver: Douglas & McIntyre, 1982.

Boas, Franz. *Indian Myths and Legends from the North Pacific Coast of America.* Translated by Dietrich Bertz. Vancouver: Talonbooks, 2002.

Bolen, Jean Shinoda. *Goddesses in Older Women.* New York: HarperCollins, 2001.

Campbell, Kenneth. *North Coast Odyssey.* Victoria: Sono Nis Press, 1993.

Carey, Neil G. *A Guide to the Queen Charlotte Islands.* Edmonds, WA: Alaska Northwest Publishing, 1975.

Casselman, Anne. "Tooth DNA Dates the First Americans." *Discover,* December 28, 2007, http://discovermagazine.com/2008/jan/tooth-dna-dates-the-first-americans.

Chappell, John. *Cruising Beyond Desolation Sound.* Vancouver: Hemlock Printers, 1979.

Clutesi, George. *Son of Raven, Son of Deer.* Sidney, BC: Gray's Publishing, 1967.

Collison, William Henry. *In the Wake of the War Canoe.* Edited and annotated by Charles Lillard. Victoria: Sono Nis Press, 1981.

Dalzell, Kathleen. *The Queen Charlotte Islands,* Vol. 1. Queen Charlotte City, BC: Bill Ellis, Publisher, 1968.

———. *The Queen Charlotte Islands,* Vol. 2. Queen Charlotte City, BC: Bill Ellis, Publisher, 1973.

Dawson, George M. *Report on the Queen Charlotte Islands: Reports of Explorations and Surveys.* Montreal: 1880.

Ewald, Ellen Buchman. *Recipes for a Small Planet.* New York: Ballantine Books, 1973.

Griffin, George H. *Legends of the Evergreen Coast.* Vancouver: Clark and Stewart, 1934.

Glavin, Terry. *A Ghost in the Water.* Vancouver: New Star Books, Transmontanus, 1994.

————. *The Last Great Sea*. Vancouver: Greystone Books, 2000.

Hagelund, William. *Whalers No More*. Madeira Park, BC: Harbour Publishing, 1987.

Healey, Elizabeth. *History of Alert Bay*. Alert Bay, BC: Alert Bay Centennial Committee, 1958.

Koppel, Tom. *Lost World: Rewriting Prehistory—How New Science Is Tracing America's Ice Age Mariners*. New York: Atria Books, 2003.

Kurlansky, Mark. *Salt: A World History*. New York: Penguin Group, 2003.

Lillard, Charles. *The Ghostland People*. Victoria: Sono Nis Press, 1989.

Mackenzie, Alexander. *Voyages from Montreal, on the River St. Laurence, through the Continent of North America, to the Frozen and Pacific Oceans; in the Years 1789 and 1793. With a Preliminary Account of the Rise, Progress, and Present State of the Fur Trade of that Country*. London: Cadell and Davies, 1801.

Miles, Charles. *Indian and Eskimo Artifacts of North America*. New York: Bonanza Books, 1963.

Nakayama, Gordon G. *Issei: Stories of Japanese Canadian Pioneers*. Toronto: NC Press, 1984.

Norris, Pat Wastel. *Time and Tide: A History of Telegraph Cove. Raincoast Chronicles Sixteen*. Madeira Park, BC: Harbour Publishing, 1995.

Paterson, T.W. *Vancouver Island*. Langley, BC: Mr. Paperback, 1983.

Paul, Frances Lackey. *Kahtahah*. Anchorage: Alaska Northwest Publishing, 1976.

Peterson, Lester. *The Story of the Sechelt Nation*. Madeira Park, BC: Harbour Publishing, 1990.

Raban, Jonathan. *Passage to Juneau*. New York: Vintage Books, 1999.

Ramsey, Bruce. *Rain People: The Story of Ocean Falls*. Kamloops, BC: Wells Gray Tours Ltd.; 1971.

Scott, Andrew. *Secret Coastline: Journeys and Discoveries along B.C.'s Shores*. North Vancouver, BC: Whitecap Books, 2000.

Shadbolt, Doris. *Seven Journeys: The Sketchbooks of Emily Carr*. Vancouver: Douglas & McIntyre, 2002.

Sheldon, Sidney R. "Eighteen Feet to Alaska." In *The Call of the Coast*, ed. Charles Lillard. Victoria: Horsdal and Schubart, 1992.

Spradley, James P., ed. *Guests Never Leave Hungry: The Autobiography of James Sewid, a Kwakiutl Indian*. New Haven, CT: Yale University Press, 1969.

Stewart, Hilary. *Cedar: Tree of Life to the Northwest Coast Indians*. Vancouver: Douglas & McIntyre, 1984.

————. *Indian Fishing*. Vancouver: J.J. Douglas, 1977.

Vaillant, John. *The Golden Spruce*. Toronto: Alfred A. Knopf Canada, 2005.

Webb, Robert L. *On the Northwest: Commercial Whaling in the Pacific Northwest 1790-1967*. Vancouver: UBC Press, 1988.

Westall, A.M. *Alert Bay and Vicinity: 1870-1954*. Unpublished Manuscript (1955). BC Archives, Victoria.

Williams, Judy. *Clam Gardens: Aboriginal Mariculture on Canada's West Coast*. Vancouver: New Star Books, Transmontanus, 2006.

Woodcock, George. *Peoples of the Coast*. Edmonton: Hurtig Publishing, 1977.

INDEX

June Cameron has sailed the coast of BC since the mid-1970s and was a competitive sailor for more than a decade. She spent six years living on a small cruiser researching and writing her first two books, *Destination Cortez Island* and *Shelter from the Storm*. She then came home to the scene of her happy childhood summers when she bought a cottage on the shores of Cortes Bay, known in the early pioneer days as Blind Creek. She has since sold her cruiser but still has her own dock, where she keeps a speedy little Davidson rowboat that she also sails on bright summer days.